Oddles of Zoodles

Your Jump-Start Guide to Zucchini Noodles

NIKKI MASSIE

ORDERING INFORMATION:

Quantity sales. Special discounts are available on quantity purchases by corporations, associations and others. Book signings and appearances can be arranged directly with the author by contacting (443) 486-2301 or info@bariatricfoodie.com.

www.BariatricFoodie.com

Printed in the United States of America.

Oodles of Zoodles.

ISBN: 978-0-9910770-3-8

Also available by

Nikki Massie

- The Bariatric Foodie Guide to Perfect Protein Shakes
- The Bariatric Foodie Holiday Survival Guide
- The Bariatric Foodie Breakfast Book
- The Bariatric Foodie Back on Track Toolkit
- The Bariatric Foodie Pre-Op Prep Kit

All titles can be found at bariatricfoodie.com/shop

Contents

INTRODUCTION **1**

ALL ABOUT ZUCCHINI NOODLES **3**

Why Zucchini? 3

Preparing to Zoodle 5

Which Zoodle Should I Use?" 12

ITALIAN INSPIRED ZOODLE DISHES **21**

Zoodles Carbonara 22

Zoodles with Meatballs 24

Zoodle Lasagna 26

Chicken Lasagna Roll-Ups with Zoodles 28

Zoodle Bolognese 31

Zoodle Primavera 32

Shrimp Pesto with Zoodles 34

Chicken Parmesan with Zoodles 35

Grilled Eggplant Parmesan with Zoodles 37

Zucchini Rollatini 39

Zoodles Alfredo with Chicken 41

ASIAN INSPIRED ZOODLE DISHES **43**

Pad Thai with Chicken Zoodles 44

Zoodle Lo Mein 46

Super Spicy Beef & Zoodle Soup 48

Chili-Garlic Shrimp with Zoodles 50

Zoodle Broth Bowl 52

AMERICAN INSPIRED ZOODLE DISHES **53**

Tuna Zoodle Casserole 54

Cajun Zoodles 56

Butter Garlic Zoodles 58

Cheesy Chicken & Spinach Zoodle Bake 59

Zoodle "Mac 'n Cheese" 60

OTHER ZOODLE DISHES **63**
Oodles of Zoodles 64
Weeknight Zoodle Stroganoff. 66
Fiesta Sausage & Zoodles 68
Individual Zoodle Frittata 69
Zoodles with Red Pepper Sauce 71
Farmer's Market Zoodles 73

COLD ZOODLE DISHES **75**
Cold Peanut Zoodles 76
Zoodle Spaghetti Salad. 78
Italian Cold Zoodle Salad 79
Greek Cold Zoodle Salad 50
Asian Style Cold Zoodle Salad 81

ZOODLE RESOURCES & INFORMATION **83**
Troubleshooting Your Zoodles 84
What to Do With Your Veggie Scraps. 86
Ruth's Banana Zucchini Oatmeal Cups 88
Resources 90

AFTERWORD **93**

true story...

My name is Nikki and I am a recovering pasta addict.

I loved almost any kind of pasta there was. I loved spaghetti (with meatballs!). Fettuccine (Alfredo!). I adored penne (with nearly anything), macaroni (and cheese!) and lasagna noodles. I. Just. Loved. Pasta.

But since undergoing RNY gastric bypass surgery in 2008, I can't tolerate noodles anymore. Any time I've tried a noodle – healthy or otherwise – I either got a stomach ache for hours or they wouldn't stay put (you know what I mean). But thankfully I've found a better solution.

Zoodles! Have you tried them? If you have, you probably already know how easy it is to swap noodle-shaped zucchini for heavy, starchy pasta in many dishes. Whether you're looking to lose weight, eat healthier, or just want a lighter version of your favorite meals, zoodles can be a delicious alternative.

We *play* with our food so we can eat deliciously healthy and lose weight.

This book is all about zoodles. You'll learn how to cut them, cook them, store them and, perhaps most importantly, you'll learn to substitute them for pasta in some classic and new recipes.

I encourage you to use this book as a starting point. While this book focuses on zoodles, you can make pasta shapes out of many kinds of vegetables. So play around with these recipes, make them your own – then delve into the deliciously healthy world of veggie pasta. **PLAY WITH YOUR FOOD!**

And that's what Bariatric Foodie is all about. We play with our food so we can eat deliciously healthy and lose weight – on our terms.

Let's connect! That way if you come up with an awesome zoodle dish, you can share it with the world.

How to stay in touch with Bariatric Foodie!

These are just a sampling of the great low-carb, high-protein recipes Bariatric Foodie has to offer. Whether you are a bariatric post-op or someone looking for deliciously healthy recipes, join us online — and play with your food!

bariatricfoodie.com

facebook.com/**bariatricfoodie**

twitter.com/**bariatricfoodie**

pinterest.com/**bariatricfoodie**

instagram.com/**bariatric_foodie_nation**

recipes@bariatricfoodie.com

In case anyone is interested, most of the photos in this book were shot on my Nikon D5100 DSLR camera with either an 18-55 mm lens or a 50 mm lens. A few photos in this book were taken with my iPhone!

Why Zucchini?

We can't start this book without acknowledging that there are many different kinds of vegetables (and even fruit) that can be spiralized. Yet I've chosen to focus on zucchini. Why?

Because zucchini is super low in carbohydrates

Four ounces of zucchini has only about four grams of carbohydrates, with two of those grams coming from natural sugars. If you leave the skin on the zucchini (and see page 7 to determine if you should do that) that four ounce serving also gives you a gram of fiber.

Because zucchini is packed with nutrients.

Zucchini's bright, verdant color is a clue that it is packed with nutrition, including:

- Vitamin A
- Thiamin
- Niacin
- Phosphorus
- Copper
- Vitamin C
- Vitamin K
- Riboflavin
- Vitamin B6
- Folate
- Magnesium
- Potassium
- Manganese

That's a lot of vitamins in every zoodle bite!

Zucchini is a great source of water

True fact: Zucchini is about 95% water. (Which is why it's nearly impossible to get all the water out of zoodles!) That water helps your body stay hydrated when you eat zucchini. In this book I teach you how to remove some of the water from your zoodles to achieve the correct consistencies for your dishes, but just know that zoodles always have more water for your body!

Zucchini are cheap and abundant when they come into season

And many of us wonder what to do with it, especially if you've planted it in your garden. You'll find for non-ops (people who have not had surgery) it takes a considerable amount of zucchini to create a satisfying plate of zoodles, so zoodle dishes are a great way to use up a bumper crop!

But don't stop with zucchini...

You know the Bariatric Foodie motto (and if you don't you're about to learn it) – **PLAY WITH YOUR FOOD!** Try out different vegetables with your spiralizer equipment. Just be sure to research your veggie of choice to learn more about its water content and other factors that may affect how it substitutes for a noodle.

TIP: Try making a recipe with your chosen veggie the first time you make it so you can observe how it behaves when cooking.

Preparing to Zoodle

Before you dive into the exciting world of zoodles, there are a few things you need to know. In this section we'll go over:

- Essential equipment for successful zoodling
- How to cut zoodles
- How to cook zoodles
- Tips for zoodling on your own

Consider this section your "one-stop shop" for making and using zoodles!

Zoodle Equipment

These products all come in varieties ranging from very affordable to very expensive. My advice is to shop around, read reviews, and buy something that's built to last – because you're going to want to make these recipes again and again!

Vegetable Spiralizer

Vegetable spiralizers are gadgets that cut various kinds of vegetables into string-like noodle shapes (think spaghetti, linguine, etc.). These gadgets are sold under various brand names and can range from as small as a hand-held piece to as large as a counter-top appliance. When purchasing a vegetable spiralizer, consider how often you think you will use it.

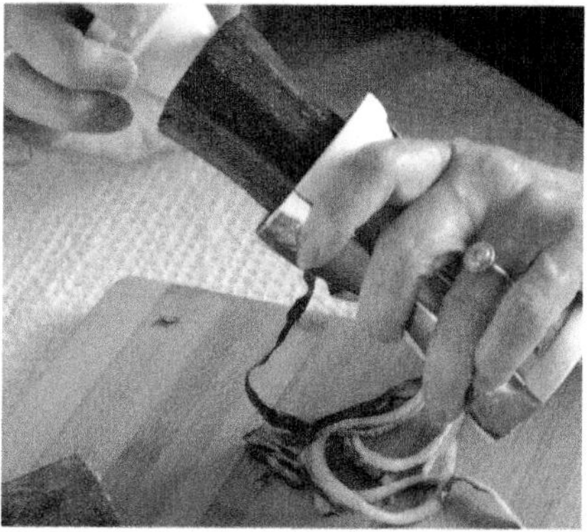

If you think you'll make zoodles only every once in a while, consider a hand-held. If you think you'll make them often, a counter-top gadget may be a good investment. Read the reviews! In particular, look for ease of cleaning (remember, spiralizers have blades and cleaning them can be tricky) and make sure your hand-held gadgets are dishwasher safe.

Mandolin Slicer

Where vegetable spiralizers cut vegetables into string-like noodle shapes, a mandolin slicer cuts vegetables into several other fun shapes. For our purposes, the most important shapes that come from a mandolin are two long, flat zoodle shapes used in this book - Lasagna Zoodles and Zoodle Fingers. Mandolin slicers need not be expensive but do look for ones that are durable, easy to clean (again, there are blades involved!), and have mechanisms to protect your hands from the blades. Mandolin cuts are, unfortunately, all too common – and not fun!

Salad Spinner

In my "How to Cook Zoodles" guide, you'll see I recommend using a salad spinner to get excess moisture out of your cut zoodles. It increases the fridge-life of your zoodles and improves your final product. More on that later!

How to Cut Zoodles

Choosing a zucchini to zoodle

The first step to zoodle success is choosing the perfect zucchini to zoodle. Here are a few tips.

- Know the maximum diameter your vegetable spiralizer can handle. In general, counter-top spiralizers can handle most any size while hand-held ones will have a maximum size.
- Make your zoodles within one to three days of purchasing your zucchini. After that, the zucchini will start to develop more seeds.
- You should also use zucchini when they are very fresh because zucchini have lots of water in them and they get mushy spots after a few days.

To skin or not to skin?

You may be wondering if you should take the skin off the zucchini before cutting it into a zoodle. The skin of the zucchini is packed with nutrients but that doesn't necessarily mean it is a good idea for a weight loss surgery post-op to eat it. Here are three situations where you should pass on the zucchini skin.

1. **If the skin of the zucchini has been waxed** (and you can tell by feeling the outside. If it is totally smooth to the touch – to the point of almost being rubbery – and shiny, it has likely been waxed), you'll want to remove the skin. Not only would that be hard to digest, it just doesn't taste very good!

2. **If you have a hard time tolerating vegetable skins in general**, I'd recommend skinning the zucchini.

3. **If you've been specifically advised by your surgeon not to consume vegetable skins**, definitely skin that zucchini!

If you aren't sure of any of the above factors, play it safe and skin the zucchini. But if you've tolerated the skin fine in the past and the skins are unwaxed, go for it! The skins are not only nutritious but very filling, which can be helpful to longer-term post-ops who may have larger eating capacities (and for dinner guests who haven't had surgery).

Tips for cutting success

Hand-held spiralizers

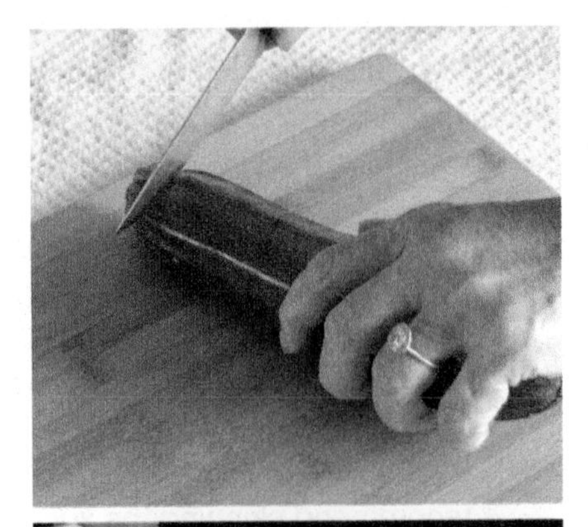

- STEP 1: Choose an appropriate-sized zucchini. The diameter of the zucchini is important. You don't want it to be too thin or too thick.
- STEP 2: If your zucchini is long, cut it into three to four inch pieces before spiralizing. The longer the zucchini, the longer the zoodle!

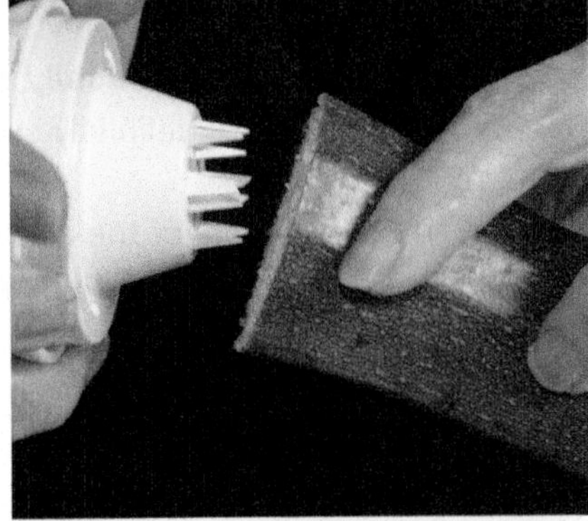

- STEP 3: Insert zucchini into hand-held spiralizer and twist it until a flow of zoodles starts. Be sure to have a bowl or cutting board ready to catch them!
- STEP 4: Once you get down to the last inch or so of your zucchini you may want to use the detachable twister, a piece that has small blades that pierce the exposed side of the zucchini to allow you to twist it all the way down.

- STEP 5: When you are done zoodling, you will be left with a small, cone shaped piece of zucchini. You can save that! I show you what to do with it on page 86.

Counter-top spiralizers

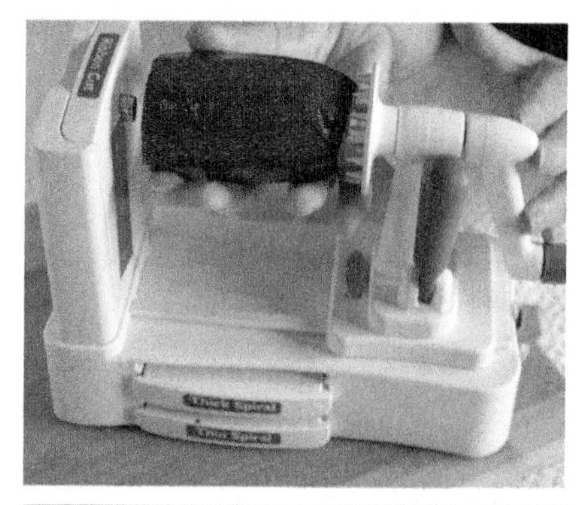

- **STEP 1:** If your spiralizer has a mechanism to anchor the device to your counter top (usually using suction), I highly advise using it!
- **STEP 2:** Choose and insert the appropriate blade for the type of zoodle you want.

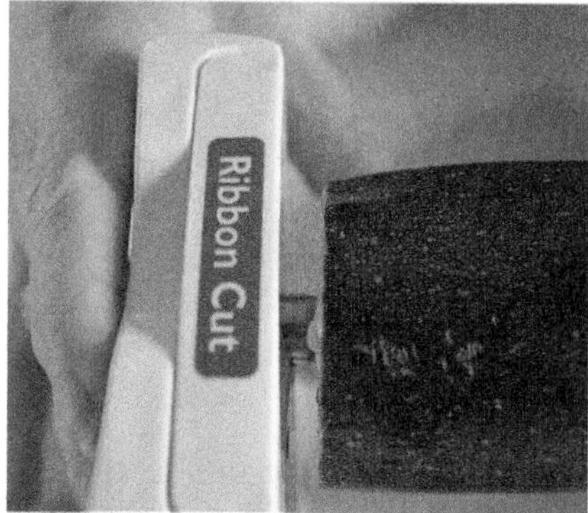

- **STEP 3:** Cut both ends of the zucchini so that both have flat surfaces. For counter-top spiralizers you can use a whole zucchini up to a certain length; however, I advise you to cut it into sections of about three to four inches. This will prevent your zoodles from being too long. Remember: the longer the zucchini piece, the longer the zoodle!
- **STEP 4:** Insert the zucchini by matching one end to the twisting mechanism (it has the little blades just like the hand-held does) and push it into the blade on the main body of the spiralizer.

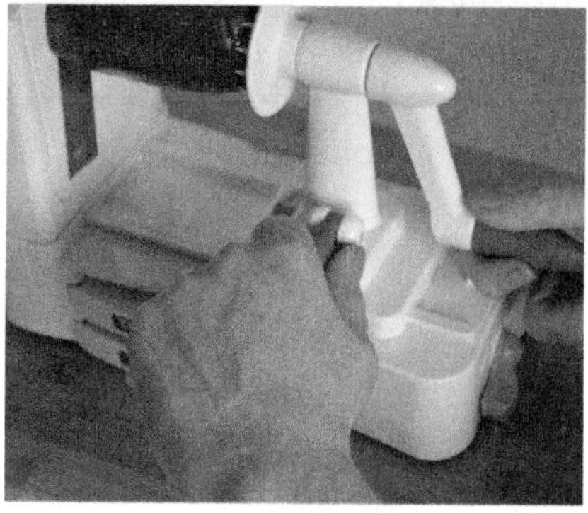

- **STEP 5:** Turn the crank on the spiralizer to begin cutting the zucchini. Make sure you have a bowl to catch them! When you are done zoodling, you'll have a small piece of zucchini with a long tube shape in the middle. You can save that! I'll show you what to do with it on page 86.

Mandolin Slicers

- STEP 1: This rings true for all the devices, but especially this one. Be familiar with the safety instructions! It's very easy to cut yourself badly on a mandolin.
- STEP 2: Cut both ends of zucchini so that both have flat surfaces. For mandolin slicers you have great flexibility in the size of your zucchini; however, small zucchini don't tend to work well.

- STEP 3: Mount the front of the zucchini just above the blade and push the zucchini in a downward motion. That should make one long, vertical slice.
- STEP 4: Repeat until you get about four to five slices per zucchini (this may vary with thick zucchini). At that point it is no longer safe to try to continue cutting the zucchini.

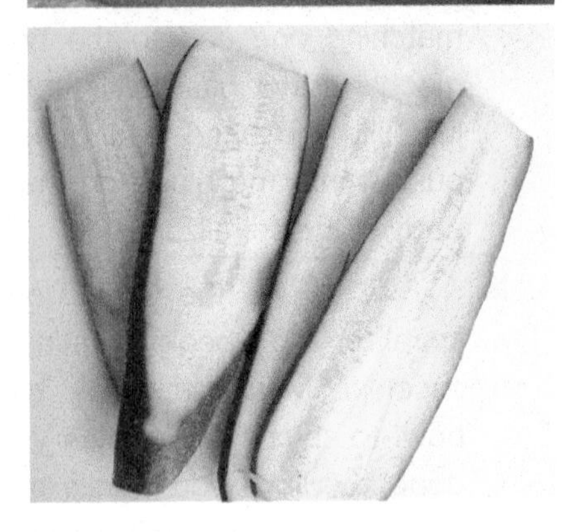

- STEP 5: When you are done zoodling, you will be left with one long, flat piece of zucchini. You can save that! I'll show you what to do with it on page 86.

Zoodle Shapes

These are the zoodle shapes included in the recipes in this book.

- **SPAGHETTI ZOODLES:** This string-like shapes can be thick or thin and can be made with either a hand-held or counter top vegetable spiralizer
- **LASAGNA ZOODLES:** These long, thick slices are typically made with very large zucchini for use in Zoodle Lasagna. They are easiest to make with a mandolin slicer.
- **ZOODLE FINGERS:** These long, thinner slices are typically made from medium sized zucchini and can be made either with a mandolin or with a vegetable peeler.
- **ZOODLE RIBBONS:** This corkscrew shaped zoodle can be made using most countertop vegetable spiralizers.

Spaghetti Zoodles

Lasagna Zoodles

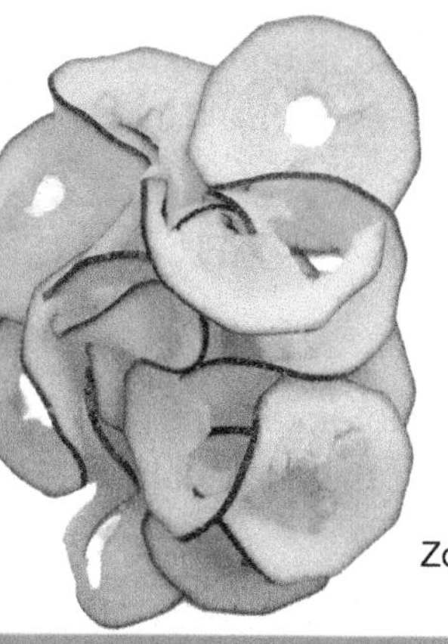

Zoodle Ribbons

Zoodles Fingers

Which Zoodle Should I Use?

The recipes in this book tell you what kind of zoodle to use for which dish but when making zoodle dishes on your own you may wonder, "what type of zoodle should I use?" Here are some tips!

Spaghetti Zoodles

Obviously these work well with any dish where you'd use spaghetti noodles. Depending on the type of spiralizer you purchase, you may be able to make both thick and thin spaghetti zoodles.

Thin spaghetti zoodles work well in dishes that originally called for angel hair pasta, capellini, or rice noodles for Asian cooking. Thick spaghetti zoodles make a great substitute for fettucine and lo mein noodles.

Lasagna Zoodles

In addition to lasagna, you can use these zoodles to do very large roll up dishes (like if you wanted to do a mock stuffed shells, which could be made as a larger version of the Zucchini Rollatini, featured in this book). Since lasagna zoodles are thick, they can stand up to thinly sliced meats like thin chicken cutlets or thin cuts of beef.

Ribbon Zoodles

This fun zoodle shape can replace many different kinds of pasta, including macaroni, farfalle, fusilli and penne. Generally you want to use ribbon zoodles with a smoother sauce (so not a chunky sauce like a bolognese sauce) and larger cuts of protein (diced chicken, etc.)

Zoodle Fingers

These zoodles when they are cooked take on the properties of an egg noodle, however they don't have an interesting shape. If you use a medium zucchini or larger, they work great with a rollatini, such as the recipe in this book.

Picking the Right Zucchini

To tell you the truth, I struggled a bit with how to describe the quantity of zoodles to use in each recipe. I don't think there are too many zoodle rules yet!

With the exception of the single-serving recipes, most recipes in this book reference the size of the zucchini you need to use to make the zoodles. Here's a quick guide on choosing the right zucchini for the amount of zoodles you want to make.

Large Zucchini

SIZE:
10-12 inches long

ZOODLE YIELD:
18-20 oz.
about 540g or 6 cups

PERFECT FOR:
You + 2 non-ops

Medium Zucchini

SIZE:
8-10 inches long,

ZOODLE YIELD:
12-14 oz.
about 350g or 3 cups

PERFECT FOR:
2-3 post-op
single-serve meals
OR You + 1 non-op

Teeny Zucchini

SIZE:
6-8 inches long,

ZOODLE YIELD:
8-10 oz.
about 250g or 1 cup

PERFECT FOR:
1-2 post-op
single-serving meals

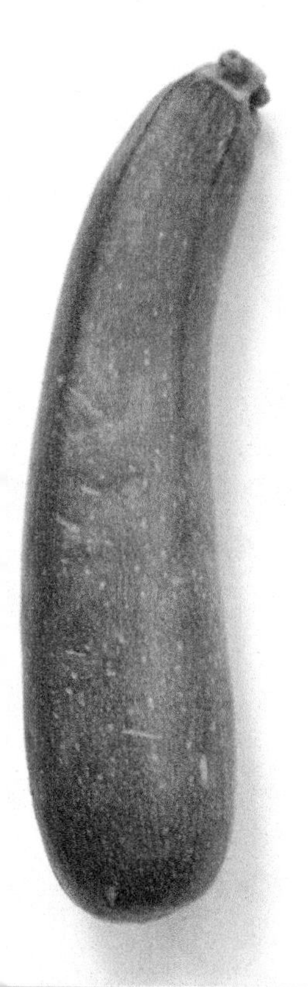

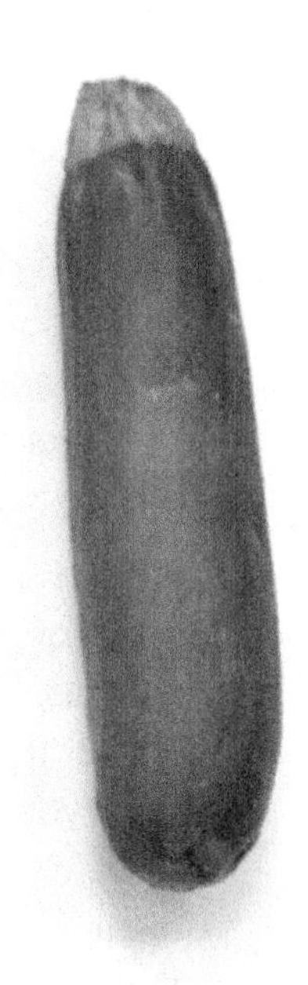

How to Cook Zoodles

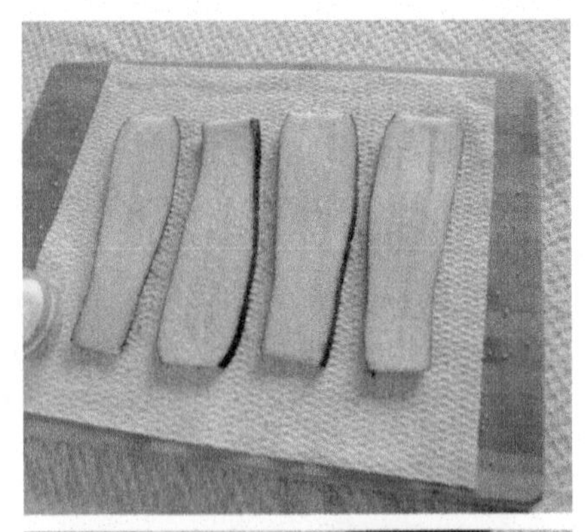

Here's some good news. If you are one of those people (like me) who never quite seemed to be able to achieve perfect, al dente pasta, zoodles will be a welcome departure! They are very easy to cook but there are some definite best practices to ensure you get the best possible finished product. Let's go over them.

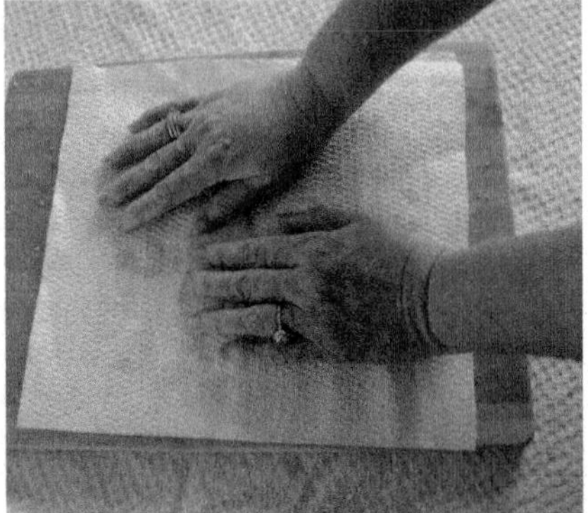

Prep Your Zoodles for Cooking

Zucchini is a vegetable that holds a lot of water, so it requires some prep before cooking for your final dish to come out just right. There are probably different methods of prepping zoodles, but here's what I've found to work best and why.

- STEP 1: Cut your zoodles using whatever cutting device you need to yield the type of zoodle you want.
- STEP 2: Sprinkle your zoodles with salt then refrigerate for 30-60 minutes. This draws excess water out, but don't let them sit too long or they will get mushy! If you're on a low-sodium diet, you can skip salting and just let the cut zoodles sit longer in the fridge (2+ hours)
- STEP 3: Run your zoodles through a salad spinner. This removes a lot more of the excess water in the zoodles. This step is especially helpful if you cook ahead. Keep in mind your zoodles may still release some water but, trust me, doing this extra step will greatly lessen the amount.

- **STEP FOUR**: When you cut your zoodles they are likely to be very long since vegetable spiralizers cut in a continuous motion until they run out of vegetable to cut. After you are done cutting your zoodles, go back through the bowl and cut them down to reasonable sizes. It makes them easier to cook and eat!

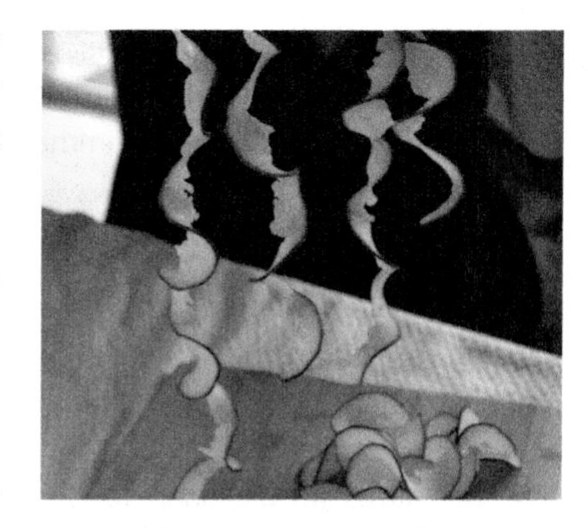

TIP: If you prepare lunches or meals for throughout the week, I would advise you not to even cook your zoodles at all. Simply cut them, remove the water, and portion them out in containers and top them with whatever sauce you are using. When it comes time to reheat your meal, microwave two to three minutes and you should have perfectly "al dente" zoodles!

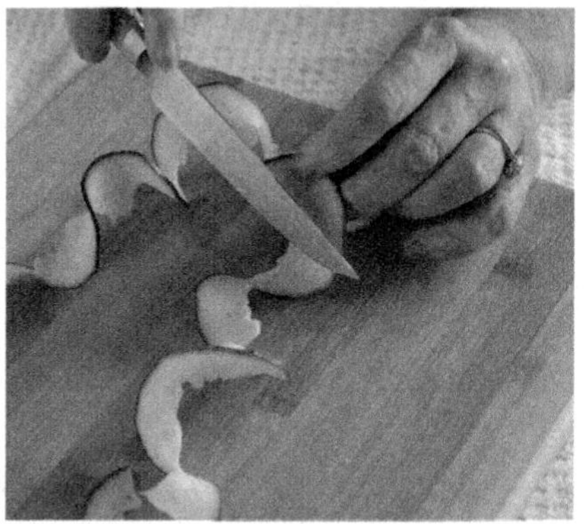

Cooking Zoodles

The recipes in this book use several different methods for cooking zoodles. When following those recipes, it's probably best to cook the zoodles in the manner called for in the recipe. The instructions in the recipe were formulated so that the zoodles would yield great texture and flavor and work well with the other ingredients.

However, if you do want to play with your food, here are some general methods of cooking zoodles.

Boiling

Zoodles are a lot easier and faster to cook than pasta. To cook your zoodles, simply bring a pot of water to a boil. Notice I said boil. You don't just want a simmer, but a full-on boil.

You can use a pasta basket if you wish or simply drop your uncooked zoodles in the pot. Remember, you should have salted them to draw out excess water, allowed them to sit for five to 10 minutes, then drained off the excess water. Now you may be wondering why you salt them if you are just going to put them back into water.

Because when cooking zoodles you are really doing what's called par-boiling (which is short for "partially boiling"). They will go into the water for no more than two to three minutes and then immediately come out (or get drained).

Pan Cooking

Many of the recipes in this book call for pan cooking your zoodles. That just means that you combine your raw zoodles in a pan (usually with some type of sauce) as opposed to boiling them in water. The sauce will help to cook the zoodles and make them the right texture.

There isn't really a special method for pan cooking zoodles but here are a few tips.

- Zoodles should always be the last (or in some cases, next to last) thing you add to your pan. Sauté all your vegetables, cook your meat, combine it all, and then add your zoodles. You may want to add them before you add the sauce. That's fine. But all in all, your zoodles should not cook in the pan more than two to three minutes.
- This is a good general zoodle tip, but make sure you don't cut your zoodles too long. Many times you'll combine the sauce and other ingredients with the zoodles using a pair of tongs. It's very hard to mix things into super-long zoodles. So make sure your length is reasonable!
- If you are combining your zoodles with a sauce, make the sauce a bit thicker than you usually would. This is because zoodles always have a little bit of extra water in them (even if you salt, drain and dry them) so making your sauce thicker will compensate for any additional water your zoodles release. If your sauce is still too thick after that, add more liquid. But remember that while you can always add, it's a pain to take liquid out!

Preserving Your Zoodles

If you like to prep the elements of a meal to cook later in the week, you'll have to store and preserve your zoodles. Remember these are fresh vegetables. They aren't meant to last a long time in the refrigerator! It's fine to cut zoodles to use in the coming days but I would recommend using them within two to three days of when you cut them for best results.

Storing Raw Zoodles: Once you have cut your zoodles, you can store them in a regular plastic container with a firm-fitting lid. They will release some of their water when you salt them. Go back a few hours later and drain them of the excess water. If you have a salad spinner, spin them one good time as well and your refrigerated zoodles should be good to go for a few days.

Preserving Cooked Zoodles: After cooking them, you may want to put your zoodles into an ice bath. Ice baths are used to quickly stop the cooking process with vegetables. Here are the main situations where you'd do that.

- If you are prepping zoodles to be combined with other cooked elements at a later time and don't want them to overcook when you prepare your final dish
- If you want the presentation of your zoodles to be bright and verdant
- If you are prepping a cold zoodle dish that will be served that day

If this is the case, simply add ice and cold water to a bowl. After you've taken your zoodles out of the boiling water, immediately place them in the ice water for three to five minutes to cool.

Whichever way you do it, when you are ready to serve your zoodles you'll want to drain them fully in a colander for three to five minutes to allow as much water out of the zoodles as possible. Salting ahead of time has ensured that there isn't as much water inside your zoodles; draining well removes the excess water from cooking.

Once your zoodles are cooked, it's a good idea to immediately season them if you are going to. Zoodle dishes can be quite bland if they are not seasoned well.

More Tips for Zoodling at Home

As always, I hope you'll love the recipes in this little book but even if you don't, I want you to have a good working understanding of zoodles so that you can use them to recreate your favorite dishes at home.

Here are a few tips.

- Whenever possible, salt your zoodles and allow them to drain off water way before you plan to cook them. In fact, you can place your cut and salted zoodles in a colander the night before you plan to make them. Place the colander in a bowl and refrigerate. By the time you go to cook them, the most water possible will have come out!
- You might wonder if you can freeze zoodles. In the making of this book I tried a few methods of freezing with variable results. The best results I had were from par-boiling the zoodles, allowing them to cool, then vacuum sealing them. Still my final result was softer than if I'd used a fresh zoodle.
- I've said this before but it's worth repeating. Zoodles are not pasta! They don't need to be cooked for 10 to 12 minutes. In the recipes that follow I only cook my zoodles for about two to three minutes.
- If you are cooking ahead (making work lunches, etc.), you don't need to cook your zoodles at all. Simply put them in the container and top with whatever sauce you are using. When you microwave your dish to reheat, they'll cook perfectly.
- Not sure what zoodle shape to use? Look to the original dish. If the pasta dish you are basing your zoodles on is made with spaghetti, cut your zoodles like spaghetti. For things like farfalle or rotini, ribbon-shaped zoodles work great.
- You can freeze zoodles. To do so, I suggest vacuum sealing them with a device like a Food Saver™ machine. Also, if you have a deep freezer I'd suggest freezing them there first (they will flash freeze there) and then transferring them to your regular freezer.

About the Recipes

Here are a few tips to get the most out of the recipes in this book.

Recipe Information

So here's the deal. Zoodles are a sort of culinary frontier. When developing these recipes, I researched the best and clearest way to indicate how many zoodles to use in a dish.

In the end I decided to write the recipe according to what size zucchini you should use (see page 13 for a sizing guide). In some instances, I advise you to use a fraction of a certain sized zucchini. In the end, this is not an exact science. Play with your food! You may like a different zoodle-to-sauce ratio than I like, so I encourage you to use the amount of zoodles listed in the recipe as a starting point and go from there.

Also, in this book I have attempted to estimate how many servings each recipe yields. This is always a tricky process for weight loss surgery friendly recipes because each post-op's eating capacity is different. These recipes all work well for next-day meals and they can be put in containers and frozen for later.

Nutrition Information

You may notice that this cookbook does not include nutrition information. In general, Bariatric Foodie does not publish nutrition information for its recipes because of the variance of ingredients available to each of us. Even a slight difference between the ingredients you have available and those I used to develop the recipe could result in a significant increase (or decrease) in calories, fat, carbohydrates or protein.

My Promise to You: All Bariatric Foodie recipes are made with general weight loss surgery nutritional best practices in mind. That means wherever possible these recipes maximize sources of lean protein, while balancing healthy sources of fats and complex carbohydrates.

In order to obtain nutritional information on this, or any, Bariatric Foodie recipe, enter the ingredients of the recipe into a recipe calculator (see the "Resources" section at the end of this book).

Play With Your Food (#PWYF) Moment

Zucchini isn't the only thing that can get "zoodled." Use your spiralizer with other veggies, like carrots. Play with your food!

Italian INSPIRED ZOODLE DISHES

Zoodles Carbonara

If you've never had this dish before, it's sometimes nicknamed "Bacon & Eggs Pasta" in the US. (Don't say that in Italy!) In addition to replacing the pasta with zoodles, the fat has been reduced. Enjoy!

Serves: 1-2

Ingredients:

- 1 slice of bacon (if using pork, use center-cut)
- 1 medium zucchini, cut into thin spaghetti zoodles
- 1 clove garlic, minced (or 1 tsp. jarred minced garlic)
- ¼ tsp. salt
- ¼ tsp. black pepper
- ¼ tsp. corn starch
- ½ c. fresh grated Parmesan cheese
- 1 large egg, beaten
- Optional: Fresh chopped parsley for garnish (pictured)
- 4 oz. pre-marinated Italian-style chicken breast, cooked and sliced into thin strips

Directions:

Cook bacon according to package directions until crisp. Drain on a paper towel to cool, then crumble into bits.

Bring an appropriately sized pot of water to a boil and flash cook your zoodles (I usually leave them in there no longer than two minutes). Drain zoodles (reserving ½ c. of the water it was boiled in) and immediately return them to the pot.

In a bowl, combine garlic, salt, pepper, corn starch and cheese with the egg and beat well. Add a tablespoon of the hot water (if it is no longer hot, microwave it to get it hot) and beat it into the egg. Repeat twice more to temper the egg.

Add egg mixture and bacon bits to the zoodles and toss. If sauce is too thick, add more of the water from the zucchini pot to loosen, making sure to adjust seasonings as you see fit. Cover and let sit for 5-10 minutes, allowing the steam to cook the sauce through.

To serve, add zoodles with sauce in a shallow bowl and top with strips of chicken. Garnish with fresh chopped parsley if desired.

Play With Your Food (#PWYF) Moment

Don't want to temper an egg? I understand. It's a tricky technique to learn! But no worries, I've got you covered.

The egg in this dish serves to thicken the sauce, but this dish works perfectly fine using just a bit of olive oil, grated Parmesan cheese and crumbled bacon. Here are a few other swaps you can make.

- If you're in a time pinch, I totally would not judge you for using store-bought bacon bits
- If you don't want to buy pre-marinated Italian chicken breasts, simply sprinkle regular breasts with a bit of Italian seasoning, salt and pepper
- If you follow a vegetarian diet, you can also use firm tofu that's been pan-fried in a combination of Italian seasoning, garlic powder, salt and pepper. Just fry it, dice it up, and toss it into your zoodles right in the pan!

Zoodles with Meatballs

True fact: I couldn't tolerate meatballs for the longest time after surgery! The meatballs pictured are turkey. Use whatever kind you like to re-imagine this classic dinner.

Serves: 1

Ingredients:

- ½ small yellow onion, cut into thin strips
- ½ of a small green pepper, cut into strips.
- 4 pre-prepared frozen turkey meatballs
- 1 c. low-sugar spaghetti sauce
- 1 teeny zucchini, cut into thick spaghetti zoodles
- Salt and pepper, to taste
- Grated Parmesan cheese

Directions:

Spray a small skillet (make sure it has a lid) with non-stick cooking spray, set it over medium heat and allow it to get hot.

Add onions and peppers and sauté one to two minutes, until softened.

Add meatballs and spaghetti sauce. Cover and allow to simmer 10 minutes or until meatballs are cooked through.

In a microwave-safe bowl, toss zoodles with desired amount of salt and pepper. Microwave one minute. Drain off any excess liquid.

Place zoodles on a plate and top with meatball/veggie/sauce mixture. Top with Parmesan cheese.

TIP: You can also make this recipe in ramekins! Simply prepare the sauce as directed. Place zoodles at the bottom of your ramekins (I suggest 7-ounce ramekins so you have enough room), top with meatballs, then with sauce. For extra yumminess (and protein) top with mozzarella cheese. Pop into a preheated 350 degree oven and cook for 30 minutes. Perfect, portion-controlled goodness!

Zoodle Lasagna

This recipe is a classic low-carb swap. The first time I served it to my family I was nervous they wouldn't like it. Turns out, they barely noticed the absence of noodles!

Serves: 4

Ingredients:

- 3-4 large zucchini, cut into lasagna zoodles
- 1 tsp. salt

Ricotta Layer

- 16 oz. container of ricotta cheese (I use part-skim; go with your gut, Foodies)
- ½ c. grated Parmesan cheese
- ½ tsp. fresh ground black pepper
- 1 large egg

Meat sauce layer

- 1 tbsp. extra-virgin olive oil OR nonstick cooking spray
- 1 small onion, finely diced
- 1 green pepper, finely diced
- Any other veggies you like, chopped, sliced or diced
- 1 large clove of garlic, minced (or 1 tsp. jarred minced garlic)
- 1 lb. lean ground meat of your choice (I used lean ground turkey)
- 3 turkey Italian sausage links, casings removed (I use spicy, you use what feels right to you! Please note that using traditional Italian sausage will add considerable calories and fat.)
- 1 jar of your favorite spaghetti sauce

Topping

- 2 c. shredded mozzarella cheese
- ½ c. grated Parmesan cheese
- 1 tsp. Italian seasoning

Directions:

Place lasagna zoodles on a layer of paper towels and sprinkle with salt. Allow them to sit 15 to 20 minutes to drain excess liquid into paper towels.

Preheat your oven to 300 degrees. Place zucchini on parchment paper-lined cookie sheet and bake about 15 minutes, flipping halfway through and checking often (you want to dry the zucchini out but not burn it).

Meanwhile, set a skillet over medium heat and allow it to get hot. Add olive oil and swirl around pan. Add onions, pepper, garlic and any other veggies you are using and cook one to two minutes until soft.

Add ground meat (regular and sausage) and brown it as you mix the vegetables into the meat. If necessary, drain excess fluid from mixture after cooked. Add spaghetti sauce and drop heat down to low and cover. Simmer until ready to assemble lasagna.

Chicken Lasagna Roll-Ups with Zoodles

Lasagna fillings rolled up in thin-sliced chicken breasts over spaghetti shaped zoodles. It's a fun, Americana twist on an Italian classic!

Servings 3-4 servings

Ingredients:

- 2-3 medium zucchini cut into thick spaghetti zoodles
- ½ tbsp. extra virgin olive oil
- 1 small yellow onion cut into strips
- 2 c. baby spinach
- 1 c. part-skim ricotta cheese
- 1 large egg beaten
- ¼ tsp. ground black pepper
- ¼ tsp. Italian spice
- ½ c. grated Parmesan cheese
- 1 lb. thin-sliced, boneless, skinless chicken breasts
- 1 jar your favorite spaghetti sauce
- 2 c. grated mozzarella cheese

Directions:

Preheat oven to 350 degrees.

Set a skillet over medium heat and allow it to become hot. Add olive oil and swirl it around the pan. Add onions and cook one to two minutes or until softened. Then add the spinach and cook until just wilted. Allow to cool about five minutes

In a mixing bowl, combine ricotta, parmesan cheese, egg, pepper and spice and mix thoroughly. Add onions and spinach and mix again.

Assemble each roll-up by laying a chicken breast out on a cutting board or clean surface, smooth side down. Spread a layer of the ricotta/veggie mixture onto it and gently roll it up.

Transfer to an 8 inch x 8 inch casserole dish. Cover with jarred sauce, then cover entire dish with aluminum foil and bake in 350 oven for 45 minutes.

Add cheese to the top and cook, uncovered, for an additional 15 minutes.

Bring a small pot of water to a full boil. Drop zoodles into boiling water and cook for just one to two minutes, before transferring back to your bowl.

To assemble the dish, place zoodles in a shallow bowl and top with a chicken roll-up. Ladle sauce over the top and garnish with additional Parmesan cheese, if desired.

In a bowl, combine ricotta cheese, Parmesan cheese, pepper and egg. Mix well.

Assemble Lasagna: Use a 9 inch x 13 inch casserole dish. Spread a layer of the meat/veggie sauce across the bottom. Top with lasagna zoodles, then top that with a layer of the ricotta mixture. Repeat, ending with a layer of sauce. Top with cheeses and seasoning.

Bake uncovered for 30 minutes or until cheese reaches desired color.

Allow to cool before cutting into slices.

Play With Your Food (#PWYF) Moment

Have you ever had Mexican Lasagna? It is "mm mm" good! But the dish typically replaces lasagna noodles with tortillas -- which still results in more carbs than you want! Here's how to turn a regular zoodle lasagna into a Mexican zoodle lasagna.

- Substitute half the ground meat in the original recipe for turkey chorizo. Remove the chorizo from the casings and brown it right along with your other ground meat.
- To the ground meat mixture, add a packet of taco seasoning and diced tomatoes (drain them first) and chiles.
- When you layer a Mexican lasagna, start with a thin layer of the meat mixture in the bottom of your casserole dish, followed by your lasagna zoodles, then smear a layer of fat-free refried beans. Repeat twice more and top with shredded Mexican blend cheese!

NOTE: You don't need to add any additional liquid to the sauce before baking. Remember, the zoodles will give up water as they cook. When that happens, the entire thing will turn out a good texture that holds together when cooled and sliced.

Zoodle Bolognese

Serves 4

Ingredients:

- 2 tbsp. extra virgin olive oil
- 1 medium yellow onion, rough chopped
- 2 garlic cloves, peeled and minced
- 1 celery stalk, diced small
- 1 medium carrot, rough chopped
- 1 lb. lean ground beef or ground turkey
- 4 oz. turkey Italian sausage, casings removed
- 28 oz. can of crushed tomatoes
- 1 tsp. dried basil (or 4 basil leaves, chopped)
- 1 tsp. dried parsley (or ¼ c. chopped fresh parsley)
- Salt and pepper, to taste
- 2 large zucchini, cut into thick spaghetti zoodles
- Grated Parmesan cheese for topping.

Directions:

Set a large skillet over medium heat and allow it to get hot. Add olive oil and swirl the pan.

Add onion and garlic and saute until onions and saute about 2 minutes before adding the celery and carrots. Cook until the carrots have softened.

Add ground meat and turkey Italian sausage and brown the meat, breaking it up as you do.

Add crushed tomatoes, basil and parsley and reduce heat to low. Cover and cook until sauce thickens and turns a deep red. Add zoodles directly to the pan and cook about 2 to 3 minutes before serving. Top with Parmesan cheese.

Zoodle Primavera

For newer post-ops this recipe might be a challenge because of all the vegetables but it's worth the wait. It's garlicky and delicious!

Serves: 4

Ingredients:

- 8 oz. matchstick carrots
- 1 red bell pepper, cut into strips
- 1 green bell pepper, cut into strips
- 1 small yellow onion, cut into strips
- 1 tbsp. + 1 tsp. extra-virgin olive oil, divided
- 1 whole clove of garlic, peeled
- 2 large zucchini, cut into ribbon zoodles
- 1 small yellow squash, cut into ribbons
- ½ tsp. Italian seasoning or Herbs de Provence
- Salt and pepper, to taste
- 12 cherry tomatoes, halved
- ½ c. Parmesan cheese

Directions

Preheat your oven to 450 degrees.

In a bowl, toss carrots, peppers and onions in 1 tablespoon olive oil, salt and pepper. Transfer to a baking sheet lined with parchment paper. Roast the vegetables until the carrots are soft and the other vegetables are browned, about 10 to 15 minutes. Remove to cool.

Set a skillet over medium heat and allow it to get hot. Add the remaining teaspoon of olive oil and swirl it around the skillet. Add the garlic clove and fry it until browned on both sides, then remove.

Add the yellow squash and zucchini zoodles and toss with seasonings. Add the roasted vegetables, then the Parmesan cheese and toss all to coat.

"But Nik, where's the protein?"

This recipe is perfect for leftover remixes. Amp up the protein in this dish by adding six ounces of already cooked protein. My favorites are leftover salmon, tilapia or shrimp, but grilled chicken breast would work great as well.

Play With Your Food (#PWYF) Moment

You ever sometimes just feel like you need a casserole in your life? (Or is that just me?) With a few simple additions, this dish can easily become your next favorite casserole. Here's what you do:

- Preheat your oven to 350 degrees
- Sauté your veggies (except your yellow and green zoodles) per recipe directions. Instead, place them in a large bowl.
- Add your cooked veggies to the zoodles and toss well before adding low-fat cream soup (you can use whatever you like but I love cream of chicken) to the mixture and stirring it throughout.
- Transfer to a 9 inch x 13 inch casserole dish and top with 2 cups of the shredded cheese of your choice.
- Bake for 20 to 25 minutes or until cheese is browned to your liking

Shrimp Pesto with Zoodles

This is what I like to call a "cheater" recipe. Not because we are cheating on our meal plans but because we are using some store-bought ingredients to save time and energy! If you have a favorite pesto recipe, feel free to use the same amount of it.

Serves: 1

Ingredients:

- ½ a small onion, cut into strips
- 4 oz. medium shrimp, cooked and peeled
- 1 teeny zucchini, cut into thin spaghetti zoodles
- 2 tbsp. pre-prepared pesto sauce
- Fresh grated Parmesan cheese

Directions:

Spray a skillet with non-stick cooking spray, set it over medium heat and allow it to get hot. Cook onions one to two minutes, until softened. Add shrimp and zoodles and toss to combine. Add pesto sauce and toss again. Warm through. Serve while hot, topped with Parmesan cheese.

Chicken Parmesan with Zoodles

If you remember no other tip in this book, remember this. **Use the meat marinating method in this recipe!** It helps your meat get super moist and tender which means less tummy aches for you!

Serves: 2

Ingredients:

- 1 lb. chicken breast tenderloins
- 1 c. unflavored Greek yogurt
- 1 tsp. Italian seasoning + ½ tsp. for marinade
- ½ tsp. salt, divided
- ½ tsp. black pepper, divided
- 2 egg whites
- 1 c. whole wheat bread crumbs
- ½ c. grated Parmesan cheese
- 12 oz. jarred, low-sugar marinara sauce
- 1 small yellow onion, cut into strips
- 1 small green pepper, cut into strips
- 1 large zucchini, cut into spaghetti zoodles
- ½ c. shredded part-skim mozzarella cheese

Directions:

Season chicken breast tenderloins with half your salt and pepper and Italian seasoning. Place them in a zip-top storage bag along with the unflavored Greek yogurt and refrigerate up to eight hours to marinate. (NOTE: This makes the chicken extra tender.)

Preheat your oven to 400 degrees.

Set up a dredging station with the egg whites in a bowl and a mixture of bread crumbs, Parmesan cheese, and the remainder of your salt and pepper whisked together on a plate.

One at a time, use tongs to gently shake excess yogurt off the chicken, then dredge first in egg whites, then in the bread crumb mixture, then repeat. When finished, arrange on a cookie sheet lined with parchment paper.

Bake chicken 25 to 30 minutes or until chicken is done through and coating is crispy.

Prepare the sauce by sautéing onions and peppers in a skillet sprayed with non-stick cooking spray, two to three minutes or until softened. Add marinara sauce, cover and simmer about 20 minutes.

After salting and draining zoodles of their excess water, flash cook them one to two minutes in boiling water. [**NOTE**: If making lunches ahead, do not cook the zoodles at all. When you reheat the dish the zoodles will cook perfectly.]

Plate the dish by placing zoodles on a plate. Top with one to two pieces of the baked chicken breast tenderloins, about ⅓ cup (or more) of the sauce mixture and top while hot with shredded mozzarella cheese.

Play With Your Food (#PWYF) Moment

Dry meat can not only be a drag, it can make post-ops very sick! Here's my super-easy, super effective secret to juicy cuts of meat.

- STEP 1: The morning before you plan to cook the meat (or even the night before) add 6 oz. plain Greek yogurt with 1 tsp. Italian seasoning, salt and pepper to a bowl and mix well.
- STEP 2: Place your chicken breast meat in a zip-top plastic bag and add the yogurt mixture. Seal the bag and then make sure the chicken is well coated in the yogurt mixture.
- STEP 3: When ready to cook, remove chicken with tongs, gently shake off excess yogurt and cook according to directions.

This works to marinate nearly any meat so that it is juicy and flavorful – and you won't even taste the yogurt!

Grilled Eggplant Parmesan with Zoodles

I started making this version when my youngest daughter decided to follow a pescatarian diet (she eats fish and shellfish, but no other meat). She absolutely loves it. I hope you love it, too!

Serves: 4

Ingredients:

- 1 medium eggplant, sliced into ½ inch thick slices (should yield 3-4 slices)
- 2 egg whites
- 1 c. whole wheat bread crumbs
- ½ c. grated Parmesan cheese
- 1 tsp. Italian seasoning
- ¼ tsp. salt
- ¼ tsp. black pepper
- 2 c. low-sugar marinara sauce
- 1 large zucchini, cut into spaghetti zoodles

- 1 small yellow onion, cut into strips
- 1 small green pepper, cut into strips
- ½ c. grated mozzarella cheese

Directions:

Preheat your oven to 400 degrees.

Set up a dredging station with the egg whites in a bowl and a mixture of bread crumbs, Parmesan cheese, salt and pepper whisked together on a plate.

One at a time, dredge eggplant slices first in egg whites, then in the bread crumb mixture, then repeat. When finished, arrange on a rack placed inside a cookie sheet.

Bake eggplant 25 to 30 minutes or until fork tender and coating is crispy.

Prepare the sauce by sautéing onions and peppers in a skillet sprayed with non-stick cooking spray, two to three minutes or until softened. Add marinara sauce, cover and simmer about 20 minutes.

After salting and draining zoodles of their excess water, flash cook them one to two minutes in boiling water.

NOTE: If making lunches ahead, do not cook the zoodles at all. When you reheat the dish the zoodles will cook perfectly.

Plate the dish by placing zoodles on a plate. Top with a piece of the baked eggplant, about ⅓ cup (or more) of the sauce mixture and top while hot with shredded mozzarella cheese.

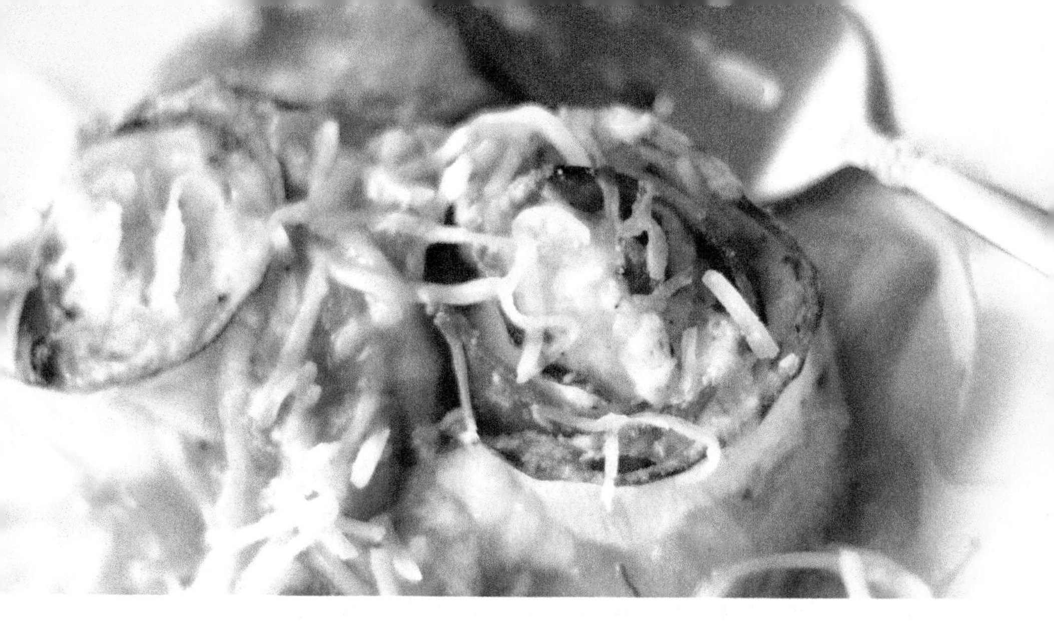

Zucchini Rollatini

This is a fun recipe, mostly because it just looks cool. Roasted red pepper, spinach and ricotta make this a festive-looking meal that's sure to impress!

Serves: 2-3

Ingredients:

- 1½ c. jarred spaghetti sauce
- 8 oz. container of part-skim ricotta cheese
- ½ c. freshly grated parmesan cheese
- ¼ tsp. garlic powder
- ¼ tsp. salt
- ⅛ tsp. Pepper
- 3 medium zucchini, cut into zoodle fingers
- ½ c. roasted red peppers, sliced (I use jarred)
- 1 c. + ½ c. shredded Italian blend or mozzarella cheese
- 10 slices of salami, cut into thirds

Directions:

Preheat oven to 350 degrees.

In an 8 inch x 8 inch casserole dish, spread out the spaghetti sauce.

In a bowl, combine ricotta cheese with parmesan cheese, garlic powder, salt and pepper and mix well.

Working on a flat surface (such as a cutting board) use a butter knife or a small spatula to spread a generous portion of the ricotta mixture onto a zoodle finger.

Top with 2-3 sliced red peppers, distributing evenly along the zoodle. Next sprinkle a bit of shredded cheese (from your 1 cup portion) over the peppers and finally top with two strips of salami.

Gently roll the zucchini slice up (some of the insides will fall out and poke up – that's ok!). Seal each rollatini with a dab of the ricotta mixture.

Nestle each rollatini upright in the sauce inside the casserole dish. Continue making rollatinis, making sure to pack them tightly against each other in the casserole dish, until you run out of ingredients.

Top the rollatinis with additional shredded cheese and bake for 20 to 25 minutes uncovered until the cheese is melted and browned to your liking.

Assemble each rollatini by spreading ricotta mixture onto each flat zoodle then layering spinach and peppers.

Nestle each rollatini upright on top of the sauce, packing them tightly against each other in the casserole dish.

Zoodles Alfredo with Chicken

True fact that blew my mind. There is no such thing as "Alfredo Sauce." It's true! (Google it if you don't believe me). Well…at least there isn't outside the United States. Here, in the land of convenience, we use jarred Alfredo sauce to create wonderful, creamy dishes.

Serves: 4

Ingredients:

- 1 tbsp. extra-virgin olive oil
- Salt and pepper
- 1 lb. boneless, skinless chicken breast, cut into cubes
- 1 tsp. minced garlic
- 1 large yellow onion, cut into strips
- 4 c. (or one bag) of baby spinach
- 2 large zucchini, cut into thick spaghetti zoodles
- 1 jar reduced fat Alfredo sauce
- Grated Parmesan cheese (for topping)
- Fresh ground black pepper

Directions:

Place a skillet over medium heat and allow it to get hot. Add olive oil and swirl it around the pan.

Season chicken cubes with salt and pepper before adding to the oil. Cook until done through.

Add onion, spinach and garlic and stir chicken into the mixture. Cook two to three minutes or until spinach is lightly wilted but not completely cooked.

Add zoodles and toss everything into them. Finally, add Alfredo sauce and toss that into the mixture.

Allow it to cook an additional seven to 10 minutes on low until warmed through. Serve topped with Parmesan cheese and fresh ground black pepper.

Play With Your Food (#PWYF) Moment

Alfredo is a perfect dish for "fusion." That is, combining it with other cooking traditions for tasty results. Try a few of these fusion swaps:

CAJUN: Replace half the chicken with cooked Andouille sausage and add ½ tsp. Cajun seasoning to the Alfredo sauce before tossing the zoodles in.

MARYLAND: Toss in some shrimp, a little crab meat and add Old Bay seasoning to your Alfredo sauce before tossing in the zoodles!

CHIPOTLE: Only try this if you like spicy food! Add ½ tsp. Ground chipotle pepper and ¼ tsp. Red pepper flakes to your Alfredo sauce before mixing. Hot, hot, hot!

Asian INSPIRED ZOODLE DISHES

Pad Thai with Chicken Zoodles

I'm big on the "make your own take-out" movement. That way I can control what goes into my food but still indulge in a delicious and special meal. This is a basic Pad Thai recipe. More experienced home cooks: use your favorite recipe and just swap out the noodles for zoodles!

Serves: 2

Ingredients:

- 1 tbsp. extra-virgin olive oil
- 1 whole clove of garlic, peeled
- 4 oz. boneless, skinless chicken breast, cut into cubes of desired size
- 1 tbsp. low-sodium soy sauce
- 1 tbsp. sriracha sauce
- 1 tbsp. creamy peanut butter
- 1 tbsp. fresh lime juice
- Optional: ¼ tsp. red pepper flakes
- 1 packet no-calorie sweetener of your choice

- 1 large zucchini, cut into thick spaghetti zoodles
- 1 c. cilantro
- 1 tbsp. chopped peanuts

Directions:

In a bowl, combine soy sauce, sriracha sauce, peanut butter, lime juice, red pepper flakes and no-calorie sweetener. Whisk until thoroughly combined. Set aside.

Place a wok or skillet over medium heat and allow it to get hot. Add oil and swirl around the pan.

Add the garlic to the skillet and cook it until brown on both sides. Remove.

Add chicken breast and cook until done through. Add zoodles to the pan and then toss well so that chicken is evenly distributed. Add sauce and use a pair of tongs to toss it through the zoodles.

Plate your dish by adding chopped peanuts and freshly chopped cilantro.

Zoodle Lo Mein

This was a recipe I worked on especially for this book. It got a thumbs up from almost my entire family (my eldest daughter doesn't like shrimp). This is another great "make your own take-out" meal.

Serves: 2

Ingredients:

- 1 whole garlic clove
- 1 large zucchini, cut into thick spaghetti zoodles
- 3 oz. carrots, julienned
- ½ c. shelled edamame
- 2 tsp. sesame oil
- 2 tbsp. low-sodium soy sauce
- Optional: ½ tbsp. sriracha sauce
- 6-8 large shrimp, shelled and deveined
- Optional: 2 tbsp. chopped scallions
- Optional: 1 tsp. whole sesame seeds

Directions:

Spray a wok or skillet generously with non-stick cooking spray, set it over medium heat and allow it to get very hot. Add garlic and cook until garlic is browned on both sides. Remove.

Add zoodles, carrots and edamame, along with sesame oil, soy sauce, sriracha sauce (if using) and shrimp.

Toss with tongs for one to two minutes until heated through. Garnish with scallions or sesame seeds.

Play With Your Food (#PWYF) Moment

If you used to love Chinese take-out the way I did, you know they offer lots of noodle dishes! One of my favorites is called Yat Gaw Mein (which in Baltimore we pronounce as "yakimee"). It's a simple noodle dish but the feature is the boiled egg, raw onions and ketchup! This recipe is a good option for when you have leftover pork chops as it requires a small amount of pork. Here's how to make a few simple swaps to try Zoodle Yat Gaw Mein.

Extra ingredients:

- 4 oz. cooked pork, diced small
- 1½ c. low-sodium broth (veggie or chicken)
- 1 extra-large boiled egg, cut in half
- ¼ c. rough chopped white onions
- Ketchup to taste

Directions:

With the exception of the shrimp, prepare the Zoodles as in the recipe. After you finish the last step, add broth and pork and return to a simmer. Ladle zoodle/veggie mixture into two bowls. Top with equal amounts of broth. Add egg and white onions. Top with as much ketchup as you like.

Super Spicy Beef & Zoodle Soup

I. Love. This. Soup! But I have to warn you, it is not for the faint of heart. When you cook red pepper flakes you release their inner heat. You've been warned!

Serves: 1

Ingredients:

- 1 c. low-sodium beef broth
- 1 tsp. minced garlic
- ½ tbsp. chopped scallions (plus another ½ tbsp. for garnish)
- ¼ tsp. red pepper flakes
- 1 tsp. low-sodium soy sauce
- 1 tsp. sriracha sauce
- 1 tsp. sesame oil
- ½ medium zucchini, cut into thin spaghetti zoodles
- 1 oz. sliced mushrooms
- 2 oz. thick-cut, deli-style roast beef, cut into strips

Directions:

Set a skillet or wok over medium-high heat and let it get hot.

Add the broth, garlic, scallions and red pepper flakes and let that come to a simmer.

Add the sriracha sauce, soy sauce and sesame oil and let it simmer about two minutes.

Add the zoodles and mushrooms and cover, cooking an additional two to three minutes.

Plate by removing zoodles and vegetables with tongs and placing in the middle of a bowl. Pour broth on top of zoodles, then top with beef strips and additional scallions for garnish.

Chili-Garlic Shrimp with Zoodles

I did not know you could bake shrimp until I reimagined this recipe. But it's true, you can! This recipe is loosely based on "Bang Bang" Shrimp (which are little nuggets of deep-fried heaven that would kill many a post-op).

Serves: 2

Ingredients:

- 6 raw jumbo (15-20 ct.) shrimp, peeled and deveined
- ¼ c. low-fat (not fat-free) plain Greek yogurt
- 1 tsp. reduced-fat (not fat-free) mayonnaise
- 1 tbsp. sriracha sauce
- 1 medium zucchini, cut into thin spaghetti zoodles
- 1 tbsp. low-sodium soy sauce
- 1 tsp. rice wine vinegar
- ½ tsp. sesame oil
- Optional: A sprinkling of sesame seeds
- Chopped scallions

Directions:

Preheat your oven to 400 degrees.

In a bowl, mix together yogurt, mayonnaise and sriracha sauce, until thoroughly combined. Toss shrimp in mixture until fully coated.

Line a cookie sheet with parchment paper and place shrimp on it. Bake for eight to 10 minutes, turning with a pair of tongs halfway through.

Bring a pot of water to a boil and flash cook your zoodles (no more than two to three minutes), then drain and return to pot, allowing them to cool several minutes. If after a few minutes the zoodles have released additional excess water, drain again.

In a separate bowl combine soy sauce, vinegar, sesame oil and sesame seeds (if using). Add to hot zoodles and toss to coat.

Plate the dish by placing half the zoodles on each plate. Top with half the shrimp (**NOTE**: the shrimp are not supposed to be overly saucy but should not be dry!).

Top with scallions.

Zoodle Broth Bowl

This recipe is partially inspired by Pho, a Vietnamese noodle soup. It's warm and comforting and can go with a variety of proteins, but I like tofu or chicken best. This recipe is written so that you can make one bowl at a time.

Serves: 1

Ingredients:

- 1 whole garlic clove
- 1 tsp. grated ginger
- Optional: ¼ tsp. red pepper flakes
- 2 tsp. oyster sauce
- 6 oz. low-sodium chicken broth
- 2-3 whole mushrooms (I used oyster mushrooms in the pictured bowl but any kind you like will do)
- 1 head of baby bok choy, thoroughly rinsed (optional)
- 1 teeny zucchini, cut into spaghetti zoodles
- Green onions, sliced

Directions:

In a small pot, combine the garlic clove, ginger, red pepper flakes (if using) oyster sauce, and chicken broth. Bring it to a simmer, then drop it down to low heat for about three to four minutes. Remove garlic clove.

In a bowl, arrange bok choy (if using), mushrooms and zoodles. Pour broth over the top and garnish with green onions.

TIP: Already prepared miso soup also goes beautifully with this dish and cuts down the prep time. You just heat and assemble your bowl. Also, this recipe works great with leftover proteins like shrimp or pieces of chicken. I like my bowl with low-sodium, deli-sliced beef that has been cut thick. I cut it into strips and put it in the bowl before pouring the broth.

Americana INSPIRED ZOODLE DISHES

Tuna Zoodle Casserole

Tuna casserole, I find, is a love it or hate it dish. I love it! This recipe is actually written as a "mini-casserole." While the pictured dish is an individual serving dish, the recipe is written to be made in an 8 x 8 casserole dish, which will feed one post-op and two to three non-ops.

Serves: 1-3

Ingredients:

- ⅓ c. chopped onions
- ½ c. frozen peas and carrots
- 1 large zucchini, cut into ribbon zoodles
- 4 oz. tuna in water, drained
- ½ c. reduced-fat cream of mushroom soup
- ½ tsp. garlic powder
- ¼ c. whole wheat bread crumbs
- ¼ c. grated Parmesan cheese (the dry kind)
- ½ tsp. extravirgin olive oil
- ½ tsp. chopped parsley
- Salt and pepper, to taste

Directions:

Preheat oven to 350 degrees.

Spray a skillet with non-stick cooking spray, set it over medium heat and allow it to get hot.

Add onions and cook one to two minutes, until softened.

Add peas and carrots and stir, cooking until slightly thawed.

Add the zoodles, then the tuna, stirring to combine. Finally, add soup, garlic powder and salt and pepper to taste.

Transfer mixture to an 8 inch x 8 inch casserole dish and top with an even distribution of cheese. Bake for 30 minutes or until cheese has browned to your liking. Sprinkle parsley on top. Serve while hot.

TIP: Now you've got just over half a can of cream of mushroom soup to use up. Use it to make Weeknight Zoodle Stroganoff – recipe on page 65!

Cajun Zoodles

True Fact: this is my default dinner when I don't want boring food. It combines several elements of Cajun food that I love: flavorful Andouille sausage, garlic, tomatoes, onions, peppers – yum!

Serves: 1

Ingredients:

- ½ a small yellow onion, cut into rings or strips
- ½ green pepper, cut into thin strips
- ½ red pepper, cut into thin strips
- 4 oz. raw Andouille sausage
- 5-6 cherry tomatoes, halved
- 1 medium zucchini, cut into ribbon zoodles
- ½ tsp. Cajun seasoning (like McCormick's)
- 1 tbsp. tomato paste
- Optional: 1-2 tbsp. water

Directions:

Prep the sausage: Remove any casings and use a ½ teaspoon measuring spoon to scoop the sausage into little balls.

Spray a skillet down with non-stick cooking spray, set it over medium heat and allow it to get hot.

Add onions and peppers and sauté one to two minutes, until softened.

Add the sausage balls and cook until they are done through.

Add tomatoes, zoodles and seasoning and mix everything together with tongs. Cook another one to two minutes before adding tomato paste and tossing through.

If mixture looks too thick, add water to loosen. Serve hot.

Butter Garlic Zoodles

This is one of those recipes that is deceptively simple looking. But I'm going to issue a challenge. This recipe can be the start of so many other recipes. If you come up with a great variation, email it to me! I want to share it with the Foodie Nation.

Serves: 1

Ingredients:

- 1 tsp. extra-virgin olive oil
- 1 large whole garlic clove, peeled
- 1 tbsp. salted butter
- 1 small zucchini, cut into any zoodle shape you like
- ½ tsp. chopped parsley

Directions:

Set a skillet over medium heat and allow it to get hot. Add olive oil and swirl around the pan before adding the garlic. Cook garlic until browned on both sides, then remove.

TIP: I love to chop that garlic clove up and toss it back into final product. After sautéing, it is salty/sweet deliciousness!

Add butter and stir until melted. Add zoodles and toss to coat, about two to three minutes.

Transfer to a plate and sprinkle with chopped parsley.

"But, Nik, where's the protein?"

This recipe is a great base for any protein you like, but especially leftover protein. Try tossing in some leftover diced chicken breast, leftover shrimp, or reheat a leftover piece of salmon to put on top. This dish is versatile and can handle almost any source of protein. Play with your food!

Cheesy Chicken & Spinach Zoodle Bake

Serves: 4

Ingredients:

- 8 oz. boneless, skinless chicken breasts, cut into cubes of desired size
- Salt and pepper
- 1 medium yellow onion, cut into strips
- 1 clove garlic, minced (or 1 tsp. jarred minced garlic)
- 4 c. baby spinach
- 8 oz. can low-fat cheddar cheese soup
- 2 oz. low-fat cream cheese
- 3 large zucchini, cut into zoodle ribbons

Optional:

- 1 ½ c. whole wheat panko bread crumbs
- Optional: 2 tbsp. melted butter
- Optional: ½ tsp. Italian seasoning or Herbs de Provence

Directions:

Preheat your oven to 350 degrees.

Spray a skillet generously with non-stick cooking spray, set it over medium-high heat and allow it to get hot. Add chicken pieces and cook until done. Remove to a bowl.

Add onion to the pan and sauté about two minutes before adding garlic. Add spinach and cook one to two minutes, or until lightly wilted. Add soup and cream cheese, stirring cream cheese until it has melted into the soup. If sauce is too thick, add water by the tablespoon to loosen.

Add zoodles to sauce mixture and toss. Transfer to a 9 inch x 13 inch casserole dish. If making a topping: In a microwave-safe bowl, melt butter. Add bread crumbs and seasoning and stir to mix. Top zoodle/chicken mixture with crumb mixture and bake for 25 to 30 minutes or until crumb topping is crunchy.

Zoodle "Mac 'n Cheese"

C'mon now…I couldn't very well give you a zoodle recipe book without a swap for the quintessential pasta comfort food! To kick up the protein in this dish, consider adding cooked meats, cut small (this is perfect for leftovers). Or, if you are feeling indulgent, you can try my reigning favorite: bacon!

Serves: 4

Ingredients:

- 2 tbsp. butter (or butter substitute, your choice)
- 2 tbsp. all-purpose flour (or low-carb baking mix of your choice)
- 2 c. milk
- 3 c. shredded cheese (I like a combination of sharp and mild cheeses – use whatever you like!)
- Salt and pepper, to taste
- 2 large zucchini, cut into zoodle ribbons
- 2 c. additional shredded cheese for the top

Directions:

Preheat your oven to 375 degrees.

Set a pan over medium heat and allow it to get hot. Add butter and stir with a wooden spoon until it is melted.

Add flour and whisk until it has formed a paste. Immediately add milk. Simmer until it comes to a boil, then reduce heat and cook another three to four minutes. Mixture should thicken.

Add cheese and stir until it melts. After it melts, cook it on low an additional three minutes or so to reduce the stringiness.

In a bowl, combine zoodles (which should have been salted and dried already) with the cheese sauce and toss with tongs. Transfer to an 8 inch x 8 inch casserole dish and top with remaining cheese.

Bake for 30 minutes or until cheese on top is completely melted and browned to your liking.

TIP: If you've ever tried and failed to make a good cheese sauce, here's a tip. If you are using shredded cheese, they include stabilizers to help the shreds hold their shape. That means shredded cheese will take longer to form a good cheese sauce. When cooking with shredded cheese your sauce will go from melty, to grainy, and finally to smooth and silky! The entire process can take 15 to 20 minutes and you should whisk it often!

Don't want to do all that? Try grating a block of cheese instead!

Other ZOODLE DISHES

Oodles of Zoodles

This recipe was a “happy accident.” I thought I had all the ingredients for the Super Spicy Beef Zoodle Soup but I did not. So I played with my food! Test this out with various levels of spices. When I tested it, I upped my salt and other spices. When a friend with milder tastes tested the recipe, she said it was fine. The choice is yours!

Serves: 2

Ingredients:

- 3 c. low-sodium chicken broth
- 1 clove garlic, minced
- ¼ tsp. ginger
- Dash of red pepper flakes (if you like things especially spicy)
- 1 hardboiled egg, halved
- 1 medium zucchini, cut into thin spaghetti shape
- 1 small yellow squash, cut into very thin noodles
- ¼ c. sliced mushrooms
- 4 oz. of diced chicken breast or diced firm tofu
- Salt and pepper, to taste
- 2-3 tbsp. chopped scallions

Directions:

NOTE: This soup tastes best when you make it the night before you plan to eat it.

In a small pot, bring broth, garlic, ginger and red pepper flakes to a simmer. Add mushrooms and cook 1-2 minutes more.

Taste and adjust seasonings as you see fit. To assemble, place uncooked zoodles in a bowl, along with whatever cooked and diced protein you will use. Ladle hot broth on top and add boiled egg.

Garnish with scallions.

Play With Your Food (#PWYF) Moment

Make your own "Cup of Zoodles!" Here's how:

- Fill an 8 oz. mason jar half-way with raw zoodles and any other cut veggies you like, along with 1 tbsp. chopped scallions, ½ tsp. dried chicken bouillon, ¼ tsp. red pepper flakes, ¼ tsp. ginger. Add 2 oz. cooked diced meat.
- When you get to work...put it in the fridge!!!
- When you're ready to eat, fill the mason jar with hot water and stir.

If you want to be super-authentic, eat it with a pair of chopsticks. Enjoy!

Weeknight Zoodle Stroganoff

I will admit I didn't have real beef stroganoff until I was an adult. Until then my experiences came by way of TV dinners. It is in the spirit of those childhood dinners that this recipe was created. It's quick to make, savory and comforting.

Serves: 2

Ingredients:

- 1 tbsp. extra virgin olive oil
- 1 small yellow onion, sliced into strips
- 10-12 pre-prepared turkey meatballs
- 10 oz. reduced-fat cream of mushroom soup
- ½ c. milk (whatever kind you normally use)
- ½ tsp. paprika
- ¼ tsp. black pepper
- ¼ c. unflavored Greek yogurt
- 1 medium zucchini, cut into ribbon zoodles
- 1 tbsp. fresh chopped parsley

Directions:

Set a skillet over medium heat and allow it to get hot. Add olive oil and sauté onion strips until they soften.

Add cream of mushroom soup, milk, Greek yogurt, paprika and black pepper and stir to combine. Bring to a simmer, add meatballs, then drop to medium-low heat and cover. Cook about 10 minutes or until meatballs are done through.

Add zoodle ribbons and stir. Cook an additional two to three minutes.

Play With Your Food (#PWYF) Moment

The thing I love about meatballs is that they are so customizable! Try traveling to other parts of the world with these meatball/zoodle combos:

GREECE: Mix 1 lb. ground turkey or chicken with 1 egg white, 1/3 c. crumbled feta cheese, 1/3 c. finely diced red onions, and 1 tsp. Greek seasoning. Roll into meatballs and bake at 350. Then cut a medium zucchini into spaghetti zoodles (thick or thin) and sauté them in olive oil and garlic for 2-3 minutes before tossing in ½ c. halved cherry tomatoes and ¼ c. sliced black olives. Top with meatballs and enjoy!

MEXICO: Mix ½ lb. lean ground meat with ½ lb. turkey chorizo sausage with 1 egg, pre-made Mexican seasoning, and ⊠ c. shredded Mexican-blend cheese. Put them in a crockpot, dump a jar of salsa on top, and cook for 3 hours on low. When ready to eat, cut a medium zucchini into ribbon zoodles and sauté in 1 tbsp. Olive oil 2-3 minutes. Top with meatballs and sauce.

Bon Voyage!

Fiesta Sausage & Zoodles

Any excuse I can find to eat chorizo sausage, I take it! This quick and tasty dish is great after a long day at work when you just want to make dinner and get on with it!

Serves: 1

Ingredients:

- 2-3 strips each: red, green, yellow bell peppers
- ½ small onion, cut into strips
- 4 oz. chorizo sausage, casings removed and sliced
- ½ tbsp. tomato paste
- ¼ tsp. Mexican seasoning blend
- ¼ c. water
- ½ medium zucchini, cut into ribbon zoodles
- 2 tbsp. shredded Mexican blend cheese

Directions:

Spray a skillet with non-stick cooking spray, set it over medium-high heat and allow it to get hot.

Add peppers and onions and sauté about two to three minutes, until softened.

Add chorizo and cook until done through.

Add tomato paste, seasoning and water until well blended. (**NOTE:** If mixture is too thick, add a bit more water).

Add zoodles and cook an additional two to three minutes.

Plate and top with shredded cheese.

Individual Zoodle Frittata

Serves: 1

Ingredients:

Equipment: use a 7 inch oven-safe skillet

- Non-stick cooking spray
- ¼ c. yellow onion, diced
- A dash of garlic salt
- 1-2 eggs (or equivalent amount of liquid egg substitute)
- 2 tbsp. milk
- ½ of a teeny zucchini, cut into thin spaghetti shape
- 4-5 cherry tomatoes, halved
- Salt and pepper, to taste
- ¼ c. shredded cheese of your choice (I highly recommend a blend of sharp and mild cheddar)

Directions:

Preheat your oven to 350 degrees.

Set skillet over medium heat and allow it to get hot. Add either olive oil or non-stick cooking spray. Saute` onion two to three minutes or until softened, add garlic and saute` another minute. Add tomatoes and then use a spatula to evenly distribute veggie mixture across the skillet.

Whisk together eggs and milk. Pour over veggie mixture and swirl skillet to form a large round shape. Immediately add zoodles and press them into the eggs with your spatula in a gentle, downward motion.

Allow the mixture to cook on medium-low heat until the edges set, then top with cheese. Place the skillet in the oven and bake 15 to 20 minutes or until the frittata is fully cooked in the center.

TIP: Want even more great breakfast ideas? Check out **The Bariatric Foodie Breakfast Book** on Amazon in hardcopy and Kindle! It's got even more family and individual sized breakfast ideas for every stage of the weight loss surgery process.

Play With Your Food (#PWYF) Moment

Make a family-sized version of this frittata recipe. Just revise the ingredient list as shown below, then follow the same directions as above.

Equipment: 14-inch oven-safe skillet

- 1 tbsp. extra virgin olive oil
- 1 small yellow onion, diced
- 1 tsp. minced garlic
- 1 c. cherry tomatoes, halved
- 8 large eggs, beaten (or equivalent amount of liquid egg substitute)
- ¼ c. skim milk
- Salt and pepper, to taste
- 1 medium zucchini, cut into thin spaghetti zoodles
- 1 c. shredded cheese of your choice (I highly recommend a blend of sharp and mild cheddar)

Zoodles with Red Pepper Sauce

I fell in love with red pepper sauce by accident. I made bruschetta with red peppers for a family function and was left with a massive amount left (I guess most folks like bruschetta with tomatoes). So I decided to try my hand at making red pepper sauce. It was one of those "Where have you been all my life?" kind of moments.

Serves: 1

Ingredients:

- 1 large red pepper, seeded and cut into quarters
- 1 tbsp. extra virgin olive oil
- 1 whole garlic clove, peeled
- 1 small yellow onion, roughly chopped
- ⅓ c. vegetable stock
- 2 tbsp. unflavored Greek yogurt
- ¼ tsp. Italian seasoning
- Optional: ¼ tsp. red pepper flakes
- 1 medium zucchini, cut into thick spaghetti zoodles

Directions:

Preheat oven to 400 degrees.

Place red pepper on a parchment-lined cookie sheet. Roast for about 35 minutes. Skin should be blackened.

Allow to cool, then peel the skin off. (**TIP:** If you place it in a zip-top bag, the condensation will make this much easier!)

Set a skillet over medium-high heat and allow it to get hot. Add olive oil to the pan and swirl it.

Add garlic clove and cook until browned on both sides (about two to four minutes). Remove the garlic from oil but don't discard it. Add onions and sauté about two minutes.

In a blender, combine red pepper, cooked garlic clove, onion, Greek yogurt and seasonings and blend until pureed.

Flash cook zoodles (two to three minutes) and drain well. Top with red pepper sauce.

"But Nik, where's the protein?"

This recipe can handle several different kinds of protein, including chicken and shrimp. To add them to your dish, return the sauce to the pan you cooked the garlic and onions in, place four to six ounces of cooked protein in it and allow it to warm through before topping. If you'd like to go meatless, try adding a scoop of unflavored protein to the blender while mixing up your sauce!

Outtakes...

I LOVE the taste of this super-easy Red Pepper Sauce. I did not like the picture so much, which is why I left it out. But here's what the sauce looks like!

Farmer's Market Zoodles

This is more of a method than a recipe. You can use whatever looks good to you at the farmer's market, but here's how I made the pictured farm fresh zoodles! These pair well with almost any protein you choose to top them with. I like grilled chicken that has been marinated in balsamic vinaigrette.

Serves: 1-2

Ingredients:

- 1 tbsp. extra-virgin olive oil
- 1 small onion, cut into strips
- 1 medium carrot, julienned
- 4 red cherry tomatoes, halved
- 4 orange cherry tomatoes, halved
- 1 clove garlic, minced
- Salt and pepper, to taste
- 1 tsp. either Herbs de Provence or Italian seasoning blend (whichever you prefer)
- 1 medium zucchini, cut into ribbon zoodles

- A handful of purple green beans
- Freshly-grated Parmesan cheese for garnish
- 6-8 oz. protein for topping

Directions:

Set a pan over medium heat and allow it to get hot. Add oil.

First, add your hard vegetables. In this case, our hard vegetables are carrots and onions because these take the longest to soften. Cook those two minutes or so until slightly softened.

Next, add your soft vegetables. In this case the tomatoes are our soft vegetables because they don't take very long to soften. Cook those two minutes or so. They may release some water into the pan. That's ok.

Add garlic, salt and pepper, and herb blend and stir, cooking about one minute.

Finally, add zoodles and toss! In this case I used purple green beans and I added them last because as the cook they turn green! I like a nice crunchy green bean (and I wanted them to stay purple) so I added them last, cooking only a minute or so. If you don't care if your purple green beans turn green, add them with the other hard vegetables.

Top with Parmesan cheese and the protein of your choice.

TIP: For this recipe, use whatever veggies you like! For mine you see I threw in some purple green beans for fun along with a few other random veggies I had.

Cold Salad
ZOODLE
DISHES

Cold Peanut Zoodles

This is a neat side dish to put out at a barbecue. It's a little bit tangy, a little bit sweet. The ginger gives it a just barely there kick of spice. Just make sure to refrigerate until serving!

Serves: 4-6

Ingredients:

- ½ c. peanut flour (see Resources section for where to buy)
- ½ c. creamy peanut butter
- 2 tbsp. low sodium soy sauce
- 1 tsp. ginger powder
- 1 tsp. garlic powder
- 1 tsp. sesame oil
- juice of 1 lime
- 2 large zucchini, cut into thick spaghetti zoodles
- ¼ tsp. red pepper flakes
- 1 c. chopped peanuts
- ½ c. chopped cilantro (for garnish)

Directions:

In a small mixing bowl, whisk together peanut flour, peanut butter, soy sauce, ginger, garlic powder, and sesame oil. If sauce is very thick, add water by the tablespoonful until it is the consistency of a melted peanut butter.

In a larger bowl, place zoodles then add sauce and red pepper flakes. Toss thoroughly, then top with peanuts and cilantro.

Refrigerate three hours before serving.

"But Nik, where's the protein?"

While this salad makes a fabulous side dish on its own, if you'd like to use an additional protein, I would suggest using one of two kinds: either shrimp or chicken breast. For the full recipe, marinate two to three 4-ounce chicken breasts or a pound of medium uncooked shrimp in ⅓ c. low sodium soy sauce, the juice of one lime, ½ a lime of lime zest, 1 tsp grated ginger and ½ tsp. red pepper flakes. Allow it to marinate at least 30 minutes before grilling (for chicken) or steaming (for shrimp). Then simply toss your protein into your finished salad before garnishing!

Zoodle Spaghetti Salad

Serves: 4-6

Ingredients:

- 2 large zucchini, cut into thick spaghetti shapes
- 1 white onion, diced
- 2 c. cherry tomatoes, halved
- 4 oz. sliced olives
- 2 c. Light Italian dressing
- 2 tbsp. McCormick Salad Creations Pasta Salad seasoning

Directions:

In a large bowl, combine zoodles, onion, tomatoes and olives. Toss well before adding dressing and seasoning and tossing again. Refrigerate 3 hours before serving.

TIP: The zucchini in this and the other cold Zoodle dishes don't need to be cooked!

"But Nik, where's the protein?"

This is a great side dish but can be paired with almost any cooked protein, especially grilled chicken that has also been marinated in Italian seasoning.

Italian Cold Zoodle Salad

Serves: 4-6

Ingredients:

- 3 large zucchini cut into ribbon zoodles
- 1 medium yellow onion, chopped

Dressing:

- 1 c. Greek yogurt
- ⅓ c. reduced-fat mayo

The Accents:

- 3 oz. sliced pepperoncini
- ½ c. sliced black olives
- 10-12 cherry tomatoes, halved
- 8-10 Bocconcini (mozzarella) balls, halved

Add Protein:

- 8 oz. each diced salami and pepperoni

Directions:

Mix ingredients in a large bowl, making sure all zoodles are thoroughly coated with dressing. Refrigerate two hours before serving.

Greek Cold Zoodle Salad

Serves: 4-6

Ingredients:

- 3 large zucchini cut into ribbon zoodles
- 1 medium red onion, chopped

Dressing:

- 2 c. bottled Greek dressing
- ½ c. Feta cheese

The Accents:

- 4 oz. diced tomatoes
- ½ c. sliced black olives

Add Protein:

- 16 oz. diced grilled chicken breast or small, cooked shrimp (shelled and deveined)

Directions:

Mix ingredients in a large bowl, making sure all zoodles are thoroughly coated with dressing. Refrigerate two hours before serving.

Asian Style Cold Zoodle Salad

This is a large batch recipe, meant for sharing at a picnic or barbecue! If you are making it just for yourself, you can use just one teeny zucchini and the same size yellow squash. The other ingredients you should be able to play by ear!

Ingredients:

- 2 medium zucchini, cut into ribbon zoodles
- 2 medium yellow squash, cut into ribbon zoodles
- 1 large carrot, peeled and cut into spiral shapes (using your vegetable spiralizer)
- 3 c. edamame, shelled and cooked
- 1½ c. light Asian Sesame Ginger Salad Dressing
- 2 tbsp. sesame seeds
- 1 c. sliced almonds

Directions:

Combine zucchini, yellow squash, carrots and edamame in a bowl. Add salad dressing and toss thoroughly with tongs. Garnish with sesame seeds and almonds. Refrigerate at least two hours before serving.

Zoodle RESOURCES & HELP

Troubleshooting Your Zoodles

It happens to the best of us. We try zoodles and it doesn't go so well. But don't give up! Here are the most common zoodle mishaps and how to fix them.

Your zoodles are too soft

This is almost always due to overcooking. Remember, zoodles are not noodles! They don't need to be cooked 10 to 12 minutes to achieve an al dente texture. Zoodles don't need to be cooked more than two to three minutes when cooking on a stovetop and should be one of the last things you add to your pan.

Your zoodle dish is bland

When I asked some friends to do the first round of recipe testing for me, nearly all of them complained that the final product was too bland. I've tried to account for that in my recipes, but if you are zoodling at home, here's my advice. Unless you have a medical reason why you cannot, it's a good idea to salt your zoodles generously. This draws excess water out of them but it also provides some flavoring for the zoodles. Also, consider pre-seasoning them (or seasoning before cooking) with things like garlic powder or cayenne pepper or any other spice you like!

Your zoodle dish is watery

(even though you followed my directions for removing the water)

One of the reasons zucchini is so good for us is because it contains a lot of water. The preparation steps I outline at the beginning of this book help to remove some of it, but inevitably your zoodles will always have just a little bit more water to give up. My best advice? When making sauces to go with your zoodles, make thicker sauces. Don't add as much liquid as you normally would. That way when you combine your zoodles with your sauce, the water released will bring your sauce to its proper consistency.

Your zoodles were seedy

There are two main things that cause this. First is that when you use larger zucchini you are more likely to experience seeds. Second, if you allow your zucchini of any size to over-ripen, it will develop lots of seeds. My best advice is to buy your zucchini as fresh as possible (I buy mine from the farmer's market) and zoodle them within two to three days of buying them.

Your zoodles didn't sit right in your tummy

Granted, for weight loss surgery patients this could be for any number of reasons. However, you may have better luck next time if you remove the skin from the zucchini before zoodling it. Especially for newer post-ops, vegetable skins can be hard to digest. Which brings me to another point. Make sure you are cleared to eat vegetables before you start eating zoodles!

Have a zoodle question that isn't here?

No worries. I'm here to help! Email your question to info@bariatricfoodie.com.

What to Do With Your Veggie Scraps

The compilation of this little book produced a lot of vegetable scraps! There were:

- Random cone-shaped pieces of zucchini from the hand-held zoodler
- End pieces with that curious tube in the middle (I'm not going to say what I think that looks like) from the counter-top spiralizer
- Bits and pieces of various peppers, onions and other vegetables that weren't enough to make another dish from

While you might not amass quite the amount of scraps I did (from making all these dishes in the course of 10-ish days!), you may wonder sometimes what to do with your veggie scraps. Well, first you want to remove the inedible parts (stalks, stems, cores, seeds, etc.). Then chop them up. Check out these three ideas:

#1 – Make some kick-a$$ vegetable stock

Not just any vegetable stock. Roasted vegetable stock. Here's how you do it.

- **STEP 1:** Preheat your oven to 400 degrees. Line a baking sheet with parchment paper and lay out your veggies. (TIP: If you don't have any onion scraps, just cut up an onion really big and roast that, too.) Sprinkle them with a bit of salt and pepper and roast them in the oven for about 20-ish minutes.
- Step 2: To a stock pot, add about four cups of water for every two cups of veggie scraps you have. Throw in a bay leaf, a clove of garlic and any additional spices you like. Add the veggies to the pot and set your heat on low. Cover the pot and walk away for a few hours. (I usually let it go for about three to four hours. This also works great in a crockpot, by the way.)
- **STEP 3:** Extract the veggies from the stock. You can do this many ways. The two that work best for me are as follows. #1 – Use a slotted spoon to remove the veggies from the stock. #2 – Set a colander over a plastic container and pour the contents of the pot into the colander, straining out the vegetables.
- **STEP 4:** If you can, you may want to can these (please note this recipe was not developed with canning in mind, so please research to see what else you'd need to do to make your stock shelf stable!) or it freezes beautifully (I usually put it in a freezer-safe bag, press out the air and then freeze).
- **STEP 5:** Use the base for all sorts of yummy soups, stews and sauces!

#2 – Make a Crave-Worthy Veggie Dip

Because who doesn't love dip? Here's a super quick and easy recipe.

- **STEP 1:** Cut up your scrap veggies. Cut them away from their stems and stalks and cut them into very small bits. Place them in a bowl. If you like, you can sauté the bits in a skillet sprayed with non-stick cooking spray for two to three minutes to soften them.
- **STEP 2:** In a separate bowl, whisk together a packet of dry onion soup mix and one serving of unflavored protein powder (optional). To that, add two cups of unflavored Greek yogurt and whisk until thoroughly combined.
- **STEP 3:** Add one to two cups of your chopped veggies (depending on how much you have) to your yogurt mixture and mix thoroughly. Garnish with parsley or chopped scallions if desired.

#3 – Make a Veggie Scrap Frittata

Have you ever had a frittata? I love them! And they are so easy to make. I'm going to give you two sets of instructions: one for folks cooking for a household and one individual frittata recipe.

#4 – Make a Low-Carb Veggie Flatbread Pizza

Preheat your oven to 350 degrees.

Dice up your veggie scraps and sautee them with some diced onion and garlic.

Spread some pizza sauce on a low-carb wrap (i.e. Flatout wraps), then top with sauteed veggie scraps and low-fat shredded cheese.

Place on a cookie sheet and bake for 10-15 minutes or until edges are crispy.

#5 – Make your Own Veggie Juice!

Combine veggie scraps in a blender with a small tomato (that's been quartered and seeded), some celery salt, fresh ground black pepper and some garlic powder. Blend until thoroughly pureed. If you don't like veggie pulp in your juice, strain through a sieve into a glass.

Ruth's Banana Zucchini Oatmeal Cups

Ingredients:

- 2 tbsp. ground flaxseed + 6 tbsp. water
- ¼ c. almond butter
- ¼ c. pure maple syrup
- 3 medium ripe bananas
- 2 small-medium zucchini, grated (don't squeeze water out)
- ½ c. almond milk
- 1 tsp. vanilla
- 3 c. old fashioned oats
- 1 tbsp. baking powder
- 1 tsp. cinnamon
- ¼ tsp. salt

OPTIONAL ADD-INS: ¼ c. chocolate chips and/or nuts. I use nuts, cacao nibs, chopped pecans and 2 scoops of Quest's banana cream protein powder.

Directions:

Preheat oven to 375.

Spray a muffin tin or grease with coconut oil or line with silicone liners.

Place flax and water in a small bowl. Stir and set aside to "gel."

Place almond butter and maple syrup in a small bowl and microwave for 20 – 30 seconds. Stir to combine.

Place bananas in a large bowl and mash with a fork (I use a potato masher). Add grated zucchini, almond milk, vanilla, maple syrup, almond butter mixture, and flax mixture, stirring to combine.

Add oats, baking powder, cinnamon, salt, and add-ins of choice. Stir until just combined.

Spoon mixture into muffin cups (I use a scoop), filling to the top.

Bake for 25 minutes (I find 20 – 22 minutes is better for my oven). Store cooled oatmeal cups in an air-tight container in the refrigerator. These freeze well, too.

Resources

Now that this book has ignited a deep and abiding passion for zoodling, here are a few extra resources to guide you in your journey to "TZD." (**Total Zoodle Domination!**)

Where to Buy

Throughout the book I mention products that may be new to you. Here's where to buy them!

Please note that this information contains affiliate links, from which Bariatric Foodie makes a small profit. Thank you for supporting Bariatric Foodie with your online purchases!

Vegetable Spiralizers

Hand-held: By far the most popular and well-known is the Vegeti™ brand spiralizer. This product is available locally at places like Wal-Mart, Walgreens or any store that has an "As Seen on TV" section. Online you can check out the Vegeti™ products by visiting bariatricfoodie.com/vegetti

Counter-top: There are several options for counter-top spiralizers. Vegeti™ also makes a counter-top version and there's also another popular product called Spirooli™. You can learn more about the Vegeti counter-top spiralizer at the address above. Learn more about the Spirooli by visiting bariatricfoodie.com/Spirooli

Unflavored Protein Powder

There are many unflavored protein powder options on the market. I recommend BiPro USA. It's very low calorie, no carbs, whey isolate protein that integrates well into most things. Learn more about BiPro USA at bariatricfoodie.com/bipro

For Additional Zoodle Inspiration

Here are my top three suggestions for carrying forward on your Zoodle journey.

- **PINTEREST:** Try searching "zoodle" or "zucchini noodle." But be warned: it's addicting!
- **PINCH OF YUM:** Besides Bariatric Foodie, this is my favorite website! Check out their zoodle recipes. Check them out at pinchofyum.com.
- **IBM CHEF WATSON:** This is a relatively new but super cool internet tool. IBM and Saveur Magazine got together and created Chef Watson, a program that can show you new possibilities for old ingredients. Get started at ibmchefwatson.com.

How to figure out the Nutritional Information of Recipes

I don't give nutrition information for my recipes (for a variety of reasons and, no, one of them is not laziness). But here's how you can figure out the nutrition information in my – or any – recipes!

The Hand Method

This one requires a bit more work, but is good for people who don't want to create an account on an online food journal. Here are the steps:

- Look at each ingredient you used in the recipe and note the amount of calories, fat, carbohydrates, fiber, sugar and protein for each serving you used. (If you used a portion of a serving, divide appropriately.)
- After you are done taking down the information for all the ingredients, add them up. This will give you the nutrition information for the entire batch that you made. If the recipe was single-serve, that's it! You're done. But if it made more than one serving, proceed to step three.
- Divide the total calories of the batch by the number of servings it made. This can be tricky. Even if you are sharing the food with other people, you should be able to determine how many "you sized" servings there are. With something like zoodle lasagna this is easier because you can slice it and see the number of slices. Or you can pre-portion your batch into containers so you know how many servings you go. Or you can guestimate! Either way, the final product is your nutritional information.

The Online Method

This method tends to be faster. Use My Fitness Pal, LiveStrong or any other online food journal with a recipe calculator to do the following.

- Input all the ingredients one by one, following the website's prompts to indicate how much you used. The benefit here is that you can input exactly how much you used instead of trying to divide portions. If you used a teaspoon of something, select "teaspoon" and the online calculator will figure it out for you. Just make sure you indicate the exact brand name of the product you used.
- Once you are done inputting all the ingredients, make sure you indicate how many servings your recipe yielded (see above). This is important in getting the online recipe calculator to work correctly.
- When you are done inputting all the information, press calculate and the website should generate a nutrition label unique to your recipe!

And that, Foodies, is how you figure out the nutritional information of any food that you eat.

Take on things that scare you, that you think you can't do. Even if you don't end up doing that exact thing, what you learn about yourself in the process is priceless.

That is my lesson learned from the production of this book.

Afterword

WHAT I LEARNED MAKING THIS BOOK

I started this book in the Spring of 2015 with the intention of it being done and ready for publication in the summer of 2015. As I write it is now nearing the middle of the summer of 2016 and the book is still not quite done! I thought I'd give you guys a brief glimpse into my not-so-great moments in food photography and the lessons I learned from them!

While I sometimes regret shouting my intended publication date from the rooftops (and thus making you all wait a ridiculously long time), I can't say I'm sorry the book took this long. I believe that all things happen for a purpose and as I reflect over the process of making this book, I can see that I had a lot to learn about a lot of things before I was ready to present this book to you.

I had a lot to *learn* about a lot of things before I was ready to present this book to you.

Here are just a few of them.

When you set out to do something you don't know how to do, it's amazing what a great learner you become.

The main thing that made me nervous about producing this book was the pictures. I had two options: I could either shoot the recipes and other photos for this book myself or I could hire someone to do it. Seeing that I am not independently wealthy, I chose the former - and it scared me to death.

I enjoy taking food photos. It's one reason I became a food blogger. It's certainly the reason I spent a cringe-worthy amount of my limited income years ago to buy a good DSLR camera.

But shooting a cookbook? That people would buy? That's another matter entirely. With my blog those are just my little notes on what I'm cooking. Yes, I share them with others, but I'm under no obligation for the pictures or the recipes to be relevant to anyone but me! But when we start talking about a cookbook - something I have sold you under the premise that it will be good - that just took my stress level to new heights!

My first approach to this was to just go out there and shoot pictures with reckless abandon.

That did not turn out so well. As I took bad picture after bad picture, I began to feel defeated. What am I doing? I thought to myself. Why did I ever think I could do this?

Stinkin' thinkin' if ever there was such a thing! So after about the fourth or fifth set of bad, not-print-worthy pictures (like the ones below) I had an "aha moment." There are resources online to learn to shoot decent food pictures. I could use those resources and I could get better.

FOLLOW THE LIGHT:
In the beginning stages of learning to use a DSLR camera, I didn't know how to control light very well. So a lot of my pictures were so dark!

IT'S HOT TO BE COLD:
Some foods don't photograph well hot! The actual lasagna pic included in this book looks like it's straight out of dinner but it was actually shot cold!

EMBRACE CRUMBS:
This was the original test recipe for Tuna Zoodle Casserole. I originally tried to replace bread crumbs with cheese, which produced a globby, flat dish that didn't showcase the Zoodles! Lesson learned: sometimes you just need bread crumbs.

LESSON #1: When you set out to do something you don't know how to do, it's amazing what a great learner you become. Sometimes we think we should do well at something on our first attempt, simply because we tried really hard. I know I once felt that way about my weight loss surgery. I felt that I should do great at living a healthy lifestyle and maintaining weight loss because I had an awesome tool to do so and I was willing to try hard.

But, Foodies, sometimes you need help. And resources. And support. And none of that makes you a failure (as it did not make me a failure to need to use resources to shoot this book). It just makes you human!

Just because the universe pushes back at you does not mean your goals aren't meant to be.

So let me tell you all the things that happened in the course of creating this book. I'll try to be brief but this is a long story anyway you slice it. It's worth it to read until the end!

When I began writing this book in the spring of 2015, I lived in a little rental rowhouse in a neighborhood in Baltimore called Waverly. It wasn't the greatest house.

LONG STORY SHORT: I owned a house years ago but the housing bubble got the better of me. We had to move. We moved into the rental house because it was cheap and allowed me to pay down debt and save up to buy a house I love.

That house came with many challenges, one of which being it had no natural light. And I am not kidding when I say that. This was good for keeping the house cool in the summer. Bad for if you want to shoot a cookbook. You may notice a lot of the pictures in this book shot on a background that looks like this:

That's a bench I inherited from my mom when she passed away. And it sat on the porch, outside, in the front of my house. Hold onto that tidbit, it'll become useful later in this story.

So I was working with what I had. Shooting pictures on the porch. But then a series of unfortunate events occurred. I'll spare you the squicky details but it involved water that was NOT supposed to be in my house and many, many creatures with tails. So I put book production to a halt. The last thing I needed was a food photo with an animal friend in it, you know what I mean?

It was at that point that I made the decision that it was time for us to find our forever house. It had been 3.5 years since we'd moved in that rental house and I'd kept my promises to myself. I paid down debt, lived below my means. I saved money. So what better time to do this?

And another few months passed as I immersed myself in the mission of finding us a better home.

Eventually I came to the conclusion that I had to deal with the house thing and the book thing simultaneously if the book thing was ever going to happen. So I went back at it. One problem: like I said, my house had no natural light!

By this time it was winter and even though, freakishly, I could still find zucchini in my local store, the days were so short! True fact: I have a day job, so I didn't usually get home until 6:00 or 6:30, which meant that the sun was long gone by the time I got home. I did not have the proper equipment to shoot with artificial lighting (plus I just love natural light photos) and so another few weeks passed.

HAPPY NEW YEAR! That's what everyone screamed as I worried about my ability to finish this book and my ability to procure a new home for my family. I did a few fun things in that time, like visit my friend/brand manager Pam (she designed this very page and whole book you are reading right now) in Michigan to give a speech at a bariatric event (while the blizzard of the century was pummeling Baltimore back home).

In February, I had some doctor's appointments for a few little weird things that were going on with my body, which resulted in me having to take a few tests. One of those tests was a diagnostic mammogram. Diagnostic mammograms are somewhat different than routine ones. One way they are different is that your results are examined right then and there (I assume so you don't go bonkers at home waiting for results). Well here's how mine went.

Tech took images and looked at them. Called in another tech to look at them. Those two techs took the images to the radiologist on-site to review. Radiologist comes back and tells me I need to have an ultrasound so they can see something up close. They do the ultrasound and with each movement of the little ultrasound wand the furrow in the radiologists brow gets deeper and deeper.

Something wasn't right.

I'll spare you the itty-bitty details but the gist of the situation was that I had developed breast cancer. It was a very early stage breast cancer and it was totally treatable. I was given two options: either I could go through radiation therapy and increased observation with about a 35-40% chance the cancer could come back once removed or...I could have both my breasts removed.

You can understand why, at this point, a zoodle book might be the furthest thing from my mind.

But oddly it wasn't. With my mom being gone since 2012, and me not having much family, for a while I didn't know what to do emotionally with all that information. I didn't want to talk about it a lot at first except with a few very close friends, so I poured my stress back into the production of this book. It felt like something I could control.

Then, Pam's life started to get wonky. As I write this I hope she doesn't mind me mentioning this to you, but I really would like to highlight what happened with Pam as I'm furiously trying to battle animal kingdom in my house, write a zoodle book, and decide if I'm going to get major surgery for cancer.

Pam's grandma passed away. And I know that grandmothers pass away eventually but Pam's grandma was special and Pam loved her so very much. I loved her so very much even though I only technically met her once. But over the years that I have known Pam I loved getting updates of the activities she and her grandma would do together, recipes from grandma's recipe box, little quips that grandma would say. So needless to say the book had to come to a halt again as Pam and her family dealt with the loss and I faced decision time in what would happen with my body. But I just want to pause for a moment in loving memory of Pam's grandma, Florence Marie Phillips (1926 -2016).

Pam and her grandma celebrating New Year's Eve to ring in 2016 together, a tradition they both loved.

Now before you go getting all depressed, things did start to turn around.

I decided to go ahead with having a bilateral mastectomy. The decision brought me peace because it all but eliminated the risk of the cancer coming back. Both my maternal grandmother and great-aunt died from a recurring, invasive breast cancer and although thankfully I do not have the genetic mutations that predisposes me toward breast cancer (called BRCA 1 and BRCA 2), I didn't want to take the risk of it returning. So that was set for early May. At this point I'd say the book was about 80 percent done. I thought I'd shot all the needed photos (thought being the operative word...we will come back to that in a bit) and Pam had done a first draft design.

OH! Also, just before my mastectomy, I finally closed on my new house! I loooooove this house. I mean it when I say I love this house. I. Love. This. House. It has a beautiful kitchen, lots of natural light, lots of space for me, my boyfriend, and my two daughters to all do our own thing. It has a big back yard for my Bassett Hound and, most of all, it only has the animals I'd like to be in it.

All in all the house was great although we experienced a few "old renovated house" disasters (all of which involved plumbing of some sort) leading up to my surgery, but by this time living in a sea of stress had kind of become my normal. I had my surgery in early May and it was successful. They got all the cancer out and I was even able to start the reconstruction process at the same time.

So that brings us to more recently (if you are still with me). A few weeks after my surgery I became antsy to just get this book done. During my down-time (translation: the time I only survived by the grace of God and the advent of heavy-duty pain medication) I did lots of online classes about photography, and food photography in particular. Because as I looked at the draft of the book, there just weren't enough pictures. Anyone who knows me knows I take pride in the things I put out and I just couldn't put out a book with so few pictures. I don't know how I thought I had enough, but I did not!

But that's OK, I went at the process with vigor. I had a minor set-back in my recovery (I think I was trying to do too much too soon) which put me on ice a week or two but once I was back at it, I was back at it.

That means what you hold in your hands (either in hard copy or on your electronic device) is not just a cookbook. It's a triumph over adversity after adversity after adversity!

LESSON #2: It's easy to think when things go wrong that your goal just wasn't meant to be. I find that's rarely the case. Instead, I choose to look at it like this. This wasn't meant to be an easy process for a reason. That reason is usually because I have things to learn in the process that only adversity can teach me (because I am hard-headed). Sometimes you have to push back your goals, delay them, slow them down. But if there is something you really, really want to do, don't give up on it just because the universe pushes against you. Push back!

I had to improve my photography skills a lot in order to shoot the photos in this book. But I still don't have a pro set-up. I kinda MacGuyver'd the cover shot. (Did I show my age?)

As I look back at that entire, long story I just told you, something occurs to me.

If I hadn't told you guys I was doing this book up-front, I may very well have just thrown my hands up and said, "to hell with it!"

But I did tell you about it. Which meant I had a responsibility to deliver on my promise. Which is a powerful motivator that kept me moving forward through so many things that were trying to hold me back.

This past year has just affirmed to me what I already know: there is power in accountability!

Now don't get me wrong, it wasn't all accountability. This was something I really wanted to do. I wanted to do a book about zoodles because I was making them like crazy and loving them. I wanted to shoot my own pictures because I love photography and I wanted to get better at it. I wanted to share this all with the #FoodieNation because...well, because that's what I do!

Accountability really is the secret sauce to develop "stick-to-it-ness"

But holding myself accountable publicly meant there was no backing down from it. I said I was going to do it. If I wanted to be a person of my word (and I always do want to be!) then I had to suck it up and get the book done.

Obviously this worked out well for me.

LESSON #3: When you make what I call a "stretch goal" you really do need to employ every tool in your toolbox to support you through it. Like I said in my first point, wanting to do something doesn't automatically make you good at doing it. Nor does it make it easy. But working all your tools - including accountability - helps to make it both doable and manageable. And sometimes that can make all the difference.

Thank You!

So lastly, I just want to send out a word of thanks. Not everyone who buys this book is a long-standing member of the #FoodieNation, but for those who are, you have been waiting a long time for this book!

Thank you for your patience. Thank you for your encouragement. Thank you for your comforting words as I dealt with the cancer. Thank you for the get well cards and the compliments of how good I looked when I know darn well I looked like one of those zombies from The Walking Dead.

And thank you for continuing to live out your journeys every single day. Weight loss surgery is a journey and it's not an easy one. Every single day, we have to wake up and choose to do better, try harder, push further to get to our goals. Your efforts kept me inspired through some very dark moments this year.

I hope you enjoy this book. You and I have all earned it!

And the kitchen is CLOSED! But not for long. Stay plugged into Bariatric Foodie for even more great recipes, tips and tricks for living your healthiest life after weight-loss surgery. Visit bariatricfoodie.com and join the #FoodieNation.

CPSIA information can be obtained
at www.ICGtesting.com
Printed in the USA
BVOW10s0510280916
463354BV00013B/16/P